BODY EGO TECHNIQUE

Publication Number 895
AMERICAN LECTURE SERIES

A Monograph in
The BANNERSTONE DIVISION *of*
AMERICAN LECTURES IN SPECIAL EDUCATION

Edited by
MORRIS VAL JONES, Ph.D.
California State University
Sacramento, California

BODY EGO TECHNIQUE

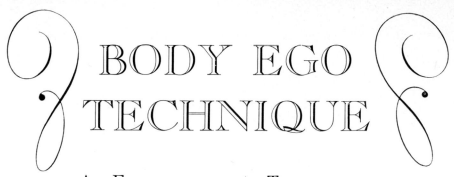

An Educational and Therapeutic Approach to Body Image and Self Identity

By

JERI SALKIN

Introduction

PHILIP R. A. MAY, M.D.

Photographs

ERNEST E. RESHOVSKY
LEO SALKIN

Preface

STUART S. TURKEL, M.D.

Line Drawings

SUSAN CAMBIGUE

CHARLES C THOMAS · PUBLISHER
Springfield · Illinois · U.S.A.

Published and Distributed Throughout the World by

CHARLES C THOMAS · PUBLISHER

Bannerstone House

301-327 East Lawrence Avenue, Springfield, Illinois, U.S.A.

© 1973, by CHARLES C THOMAS · PUBLISHER

ISBN 0–398–02826–5

Library of Congress Catalog Card Number: 73–214

*With THOMAS BOOKS careful attention is given to all details of
manufacturing and design. It is the Publisher's desire to present books that are
satisfactory as to their physical qualities and artistic possibilities and
appropriate for their particular use. THOMAS BOOKS will be true to those
laws of quality that assure a good name and good will.*

TO MY DAUGHTER LYNN

FOREWORD

I AM OFTEN ASKED how I, a dancer, became involved in Body Ego Technique and how this technique came into being.

I danced, as all children do, throughout my childhood. However, I loved to dance so much that it became a way of life for me. I found comfort in dance, I found escape in dance and I found fun and excitement in dance. I could be happy or sad, pretend to be anyone or anything just by changing the way I danced.

Much later I learned that dance had been used since the beginning of time for similar reasons.

Only now, after years of experience, can I look back and see how dance has moulded my life. Only now can I clearly understand the beneficial, educational and therapeutic values that are a part of dance. Only now can I appreciate the important influence that dance can have upon the maturity or the lack of maturity of an individual. And only now can I explain how to use dance most effectively, other than by performing.

Soon after I finished high school I had the opportunity to meet Lester Horton, a prominent choreographer, and to become a member of his professional dance group. One of the contributing factors to my knowledge and ability to be able now to break down and use the separate elements of dance was my extensive theatrical training. I took as many as five modern dance classes a day, was exposed to and learned other forms of dance such as ballet, toe, Spanish, Indian, folk dance and mime. I studied art history, dance history, theatrical lighting, make-up and how to make costumes. I studied composition and choreography and learned how to teach dance.

I became aware that as I experienced changes in movements, regardless of the content of the dance, these changes actually caused me to feel differently about myself and my environment and seemed to have an effect upon my behavior.

Because I was especially fond of and seemed to have rapport with children of all ages I became the teacher, director, and the choreographer of The Lester Horton Children's Dance School. During the eleven years of performing with the Lester Horton Dance Group, and for the many years following, I have specialized in working with children.

By carefully observing the children I was teaching, I concluded that there was visible evidence of the relationship between their body posture, muscle tone, physical skill, learning potential, eye focus, individual rhythmic patterns and their overall behavior. I did not realize at the time that I was dealing with their sense of body image, or lack of it, or their sense of individual identity, or lack of it.

When I approached the children at the developmental level where they were functioning, it seemed easier to teach them to broaden their range of movement, their range of thought and their range of balanced behavior. Their skill achievement, their physical and emotional confidence and their ability to communicate seemed to develop at parallel levels.

These children were considered to be average or normal, both by their families and school teachers. However, there did seem to be a large number of them whose behavior indicated that they had some developmental lags. Whether these problems were minor or extreme, normal or abnormal, the dance classes seemed to change and improve their behavior and their ability to learn.

Because I too had experienced the beneficial effects of dance, I realized that the elements of this performing art had both educational and therapeutic values.

When teaching dance to young children or to beginners of any age, the various components of movement have to be separated, simplified, emphasized, exaggerated and then organized. When these simple forms are given purposeful content, a set rhythm, a space pattern and learned so that they can be repeated, a simple dance has been created.

When children or adults have exaggerated psychological problems, it seems that they lose their individual sense of identity and they have confused body boundaries and body images. Dance seems, in my opinion, to be a direct approach in helping to establish or to reestablish these necessary aspects of balanced behavior.

I was fascinated, enthusiastic and excited about the knowledge that this art form that was so satisfying to experience held within it developmental, educational, diagnostic and therapeutic values, not only for children but for all individuals. I wanted to learn more about these. When I stopped performing I continued to teach, explore and learn. For seven of the years while teaching normal children to learn about themselves through dance, I also taught classes to children and adults at Camarillo State Hospital. At first I volunteered one day a week and later, through a research grant from the State of California Department of Mental Hygiene, I taught there every day.

The chief of research at the hospital pointed out to me that I was not teaching "Dance Therapy" such as folk dance, social dance, recreational dance nor the usually accepted form of expressive dance. He helped me to understand that I was really using the separate elements of dance or movement in various ways to develop a *technique* that used the *body* posture and movement changes to help develop the *ego*. I was at first reluctant to accept this Body Ego Technique title because I thought perhaps it would eliminate dance. I then realized that I had been, for a long time, teaching this way when working with educational, nonprofessional and children's dance. I agreed that it was a more precise all-encompassing name.

All individuals, including dancers, must develop a sense of identity and establish a body image. Body Ego Technique attempts, in one way or another, to accomplish these for the developing young child, the older child, the adult, the teacher, the professional dancer and for the psychiatric patient, through this special approach and use of the elements of dance.

As a result of my experience as a performing artist, as a teacher, as a choreographer and as a therapist, I believe that in every phase of life, at every age of life, the one most important need is for each individual to establish a sense of *identity*. The one most important developmental accomplishment of the young child is to gain a sense of separateness and *identity*. The one most important contribution to the student for scholastic achievement is his ability to maintain a sense of individual *identity*. The one most important attribute of a good teacher is a sense of *identity*. The one outstanding loss for the mentally ill is the loss of his *identity*. And, the one most important ability that the performing artist must have is to be able to separate his real sense of *identity* from his make-believe role *identity*. The one most important quality that keeps the elderly alert and active is a sense of *identity*. And so, the basic objective is the same for all individuals—to establish or reestablish or to maintain and then utilize the clear sense of *body image* and *self-identity*. The approach of the dance or Body Ego Technique teacher, before and after this step is accomplished, is dependent upon the age, the condition, development, and the final objectives of the individuals involved in the specific class.

BODY IMAGE AND IDENTITY

Body Image is the picture or mental representation one has of his own body at rest or in motion at any moment. It is derived from internal sensations, postural changes, contact with outside objects and people, emotional experiences and fantasies.*

The sense of a body image begins to develop some time during the last half of the first year of life. At that time it is largely unconscious. Body image becomes more evident as an individual begins to develop a sense of self-identity. Self or personal identity is the unity of personality over a period of time. Milton Wexler has stated:

. . . body image seems intimately linked with the problem of personal identity which is so central to the psychological stability of the organism.†

When one is stable, his behavior is not given to extreme swings in mood nor does he function by showing marked changes in his emotional attitude. In other words, his affect (emotional response) is congruent with what would normally be expected in a given situation.

An infant or young child does not function with much stability or balance. During the first few months of life, the baby does not have an identity or a body image. A baby is not born with perception nor with functioning

* English and English Dictionary of psychological and psychoanalytical terms. Horace B. English and Ava C. English: A *Comprehensive Dictionary of Psychological and Psychoanalytical Terms*. A Guide to Usage. 1st Ed. New York. Longmans, Green 1958. Pg. 70.

† Milton Wexler, personal communication.

creativity and he is not born physically proficient. If an infant is denied tactile experiences, postural changes, contact with outside objects and people, emotional experiences and fantasies, he will not grow or develop normally. He will not establish a body image. He will not gain a sense of individual identity. Indeed he may not survive. Most individuals have enough of these experiences to allow them to grow and develop to an adult age, but complete maturity with constantly stable behavior is rare in the human species.

Given this assumption, it seems that it is not only important but absolutely necessary to attempt to establish or reestablish body image and personal identity regardless of age or condition. In order to establish and maintain this important asset, much help is needed, for the healthy newborn infant as well as for the more disturbed older individual.

In Body Ego Technique, this is the first, the fundamental, the prime objective. Some awareness of body image and identity is necessary before other elements of movement can be organized to any functional degree and before speech or academic learning can begin.

This should be taught as a routine part of every individual's education. The infant can learn from the mother or mother substitute. It can be taught in day care centers and nursery schools, in elementary schools, junior high and high schools and in the universities and elsewhere. Body Ego Technique can be used as dance or movement education, preventive therapy or rehabilitation therapy as well as a preparation for a professional career.

The organization of the rhythm and the quality of the purposeful goal-directed movements of Body Ego Technique distinguish this technique as originating in and striving towards an art form and should not be confused with the organization and objectives of the physical activity used in gymnastics, physical education or games. Other art forms such as drawing, painting and music have been integrated into the educational system and have been taught to children on a nonprofessional level without losing their artistic values or professional identity. It should also be possible to use the elements of the art of professional performing dance without teaching the profession but not ignoring its existence. Webster's dictionary defines Art as:

> Skill in performance, acquired by experience, study or observation; Systematic application of knowledge or skill effecting a desired result; Art is often used interchangeably with skill when both imply proficiency or expertness in the exercise or practical application of knowledge.

Knowledge and skill are being acquired at various ages and at different levels of expertness throughout one's lifetime. The systematic application of knowledge or skill in effecting a desired result cannot take place to its fullest degree until after one has developed many separate skills and has gained a broad knowledge of the elements that help to establish a sense of identity and a clear body image. The sophistication, the abstraction, the aesthetic (good taste) and the communication of the artist with an audience must come much later to the individual who has chosen a professional career in dance.

When teaching Body Ego Technique the instructor is helping to organize, give form and discipline to external movement patterns. By broadening and changing the external movement organization, discipline and form, the internal emotional experiences and fantasies are also broadened. The range of stable behavior broadens as one's real or assimilated experiences broaden. A conscious awareness of how to externally express internal thoughts and conflicts through movement brings about much relief, satisfaction and a sense of well-being. It is fun to move and every child as well as every well-balanced adult enjoys moving, whether they call it dance or play or work.

PREFACE

CLINICAL ASPECTS OF
BODY EGO TECHNIQUE

IN ORDER TO understand Body Ego Technique, both as an area of scientific exploration and as a therapeutic modality, it is necessary to have an appreciation of some of the physiological and psychological factors that initiate and impinge on voluntary muscle movements. Even the simplest movement involves a complex series of physiological and psychological components that are integrated outside of mental awareness. This is not because of any lack of attention or psychological repression, but is a function of brain structure and physiology. It is this aspect of physiological functioning that allows us to use our limbs and bodies as the instruments of our desires. The faculties involved in mental concentration and will would otherwise be hopelessly mired in the welter of ongoing physiological functions necessary for movement and life. Voluntary muscle movements, postures and degrees of muscle tone take place within and outside of awareness. Furthermore, voluntary muscle responses often enough are without voluntary control even in the presence of conscious awareness. The voluntary musculature is very responsive to states of mind in various nonspecific ways and in ways which are representational or symbolic of ideational content. Thus within the confines of anatomy and physiology there is a wide range of emotional life expressed through the musculature.

Ordinarily speaking, the awareness and attributing of content is most frequently applied to the facial muscles. After this, one is aware of the utilization of gestures, both large and small, general body postures, and various uncontrolled tremors and movements of the body, in terms of emotional and ideational content. After these areas there is a whole body of information more easily read by the intuitive, highly trained and skilled dancers because of their use of movement as communication. Patterns of locomotion, abilities to perform various movements, degrees of muscle tone, disparities in muscle tone between body areas, exaggerations and restrictions of conscious and unconscious expressive movements; all are much more fully appreciated by the highly trained dancer.

Various muscle functions and the patterning necessary to achieve these functions are initially and largely determined by physiological potentials that are inborn and that continue to mature and develop throughout the early years of life. There is no question, though, that from birth on the musculature is very responsive to the individual's state of mind. Thus, there is a psychological component both influential in the initiation and then superimposed on every aspect of muscle function. Eating, walking, standing, sleeping, loving, excreting, etc. are initiated, colored and influenced by emotional factors and are in turn expressive of various emotional components that are conscious and unconscious.

There are areas of muscle function and response which are much less explored and understood. One such area is the question of how and in what ways the responses themselves become reinforcing and awareness-producing factors with respect to the conflict and emotion that initiated them. Another area is the question of whether the responses can, as a function of degree and time and initial content, become self-perpetuating so that they no longer need the same degree of emotion or conflict (perhaps maybe even in the absence of such emotional conflict) to continue to exist. In this type of situation the muscle responses can be understood to maintain a significant degree of emotional tone or informational feedback even though the individual, without the muscle response, would no longer feel the same way. It is in this area that we see the utilization of various relaxing and desensitization techniques which can be helpful in dealing with general feelings of tension, anxiety and problems of phobias. The palpitating heart, the tremulous hand, the shaky body, the restrictions and constrictions of muscular movement all have their feedback influence on the human mind.

Perhaps the most interesting area and the one which is most important to the work of Body Ego Technique is the area of therapeutic efficacy involved in making the person aware of various bodily tensions and movements while at the same time helping the individual to initiate postures and movements which of necessity must touch on psychological conflicts and ways of responding because of their representational or symbolic content. In helping an individual to become aware of his body musculature along with the initiation of postures and movements which have been distorted through tension and conflict, the technique of necessity causes the individual to come to grips in some nonverbal fashion with some of the emotions and with their consequences with respect to movement, posture and tone. The question then is how much and in what ways can the study and utilization of body movement be useful both in helping the individual become aware of and, in some way, able to deal more effectively with sexual, aggressive and other feelings which have been locked into physical patterns of movement, tone and physical posture. It is to this end that the book addresses itself and it is to this end that Body Ego Technique is utilized therapeutically.

My experience with Body Ego Technique has been extensive, encompassing over ten years the original research and study project at Camarillo State Hospital and its continuing development and utilization on the Psychiatric Inpatient Service of the Cedars-Sinai Medical Center in Los Angeles.

There is no question that the "art of therapy" is very important in the use of this modality. This factor is important in any form of psychological therapy but particularly so where nonverbal movement components predominate. Mrs. Salkin brings to the technique a very high degree of maturity, intellectual discipline and long experience working in a dynamically oriented psychiatric setting. The success of her work is thus significantly influenced by her manner and expertise in working with patients. She has, though, developed a significant body of organized information that allows the technique to be taught to others. Her assistants and students are able to duplicate her work in an intelligent fashion. This is very important as a measure of the reality of her work as a transmittable body of knowledge. Furthermore, therapists in this general area who do not utilize her approach do not, in my experience, achieve similar results.

The Inpatient Service at Cedars-Sinai Medical Center is a self-contained unit in a general hospital with large training and research programs. Most of the patients are of upper-middle and wealthy economic status but the clinic patients are drawn from families without the financial resources to afford the expense of an intensive psychiatric program. The treatment program is extensive and closely supervised and coordinated, with Body Ego Technique being one of the treatment modalities.

It is remarkable to observe how patients with various problems and moods almost always respond in a markedly favorable manner. Patients who are depressed, anxious, withdrawn, and/or confused become involved with Mrs. Salkin and then with others in the group in an obviously enjoyable and contemplative manner. The introspective aspect is very important for it is in the integration of experiencing an inner awareness of meaning that gives any therapy its lasting qualities. As a group session proceeds, patients begin to move more normally, become more animated, take appropriate account of others, become spontaneous, chat, and report about themselves. In subsequent sessions progressive improvement can be easily observed. Inasmuch as recovery takes place in a context of an intensive treatment program, there is no way presently to determine the singular role of Body Ego Technique. At present I can only comment on our clinical observation of dramatic patient responsiveness in Body Ego Technique sessions.

Finally, it is important to note the absence of childish self-indulgence, mystique or artificial dramatics. This allows for psychological integration at a level of personal exchange consistent with adult relationships in daily life.

Stuart S. Turkel, M.D.

Chief, Adult and Adolescent Inpatient Services
Division of Psychiatry and
Thalians Community Mental Health Center
Cedars-Sinai Medical Center
Los Angeles, California

Fellow American Psychiatric Association
Member Southern California Psychoanalytic Institute

INTRODUCTION
BODY EGO, BODY IMAGE AND
SELF IDENTITY

I TAKE particular pleasure in having had the opportunity to read the manuscript of this book before it went to press, because it develops systematically and in detail the educational aspects of an approach that I have encouraged and helped since 1958, as a unique and exciting application of the knowledge and insights of modern dance theory to research and development in the mental health field.

It is also very much in line with modern psychodynamic psychology. Freud placed great emphasis on the physical body as the basis of the ego. He saw that the ego is first and foremost a body ego. Its mental representations, the body image and sense of identity, must derive from bodily sensations, since every new experience can enter only through the body and must somehow be related to it. Thus, in the final analysis, the body ego is the fundamental basis for object relationships.

The central importance of body image in the normal development and maintenance of ego identity and reality perception was further elaborated by Schilder and others. The infant at the breast does not distinguish himself from his mother's body. At this early stage, one can hardly talk of an ego, for there is no distinction between 'self' and 'not self.' Gradually a person emerges from this primary identification with surrounding objects. The child must learn that he has a separate body from his mother, that he has separate body boundaries, that he has an identity, and he must learn how he relates to other objects in space. Without such mental representations of the self, there can be no adequate differentiation from the outside world. Awareness of the distinction between 'self' and 'not self' is the subjective aspect of developing ego boundaries, and a prerequisite for secondary identification with parents, teachers and others.

Clinicians such as Schilder, Hoffer, Fenichel, Federn, Scott, Freedman, Greenson, Jacobson, Bellak, DesLauriers, and Freeman, Cameron, and McGhie, have drawn attention to the fact that disturbances of body image produce disruption and arrest in psychic structure, especially in those areas of ego functioning which have to do with reality relationships.

This is especially prominent in psychosis. Psychotic object-relationship disturbances include misidentifications, failure of self-other discrimination, and merging of the self with others. Such patients have a poorly integrated sense of self with all sorts of extraordinary concepts of what is good and bad about themselves and others. Indeed, dissolution of body ego boundaries and of relationships between self and object is now widely conceptualized as a basic disturbance in schizophrenia, of which all other manifestations may be purely secondary elaborations. In this context, the process of recovery in schizophrenia can be seen as a progressive definition and demarcation of the patient's ego boundaries, through a systematically increased cathexis of his bodily limits and his bodily self.

Clearly, if the schizophrenic or the normal child is confused about the limits of his own body, attempts to help him define and identify those limits are worth exploring. In fact, definition of these limits might even in some instances be a necessary prerequisite for other attempts to build and strengthen the ego. One possible way of doing this would be through reeducational attempts to reestablish the experience of the bodily self as differentiated, bounded, and separated from the non-self, using techniques that would make available to the schizophrenic experiences, sensations, feelings, images, movements, needs and affects connected with his own body.

In retrospect, it is curious that there have been relatively few attempts to make deliberate use of these concepts. Treatment and educational techniques tend to be heavily verbal. Although an approach concentrating on body image, identity, posture and movement has been strongly advocated by research clinicians such as Bellak, DesLauriers and Fisher and Cleveland, interest in specific treatment of this sort has been limited. Even techniques such as art therapy, occupational therapy, work therapy and corrective or physical therapy usually define their goals in terms of sublimation and discharge of instinctual energy, socialization or rehabilitation rather than nonverbal contact or deliberate reintegration of body image and identity. This general neglect is surprising since one might imagine that methods of treatment that are relatively nonverbal would pay particular attention to body ego.

Dance therapists have also tended to focus on emotional self-expression and communication or improvement of physical coordination and socialization with, at the most, only a marginal attention to body awareness or change in body image. The possibility of change in these areas has been recognized by some, but not the potential for systematic focus as an educational approach.

Jeri Salkin develops this body-ego theme from her viewpoint as a modern dancer, starting with an outline of the underlying concepts and the relationship of Body Ego Technique to early childhood development. In subsequent chapters, she discusses the fundamental elements that are employed in her approach—movement, form, space and rhythm—how they may be used by the teacher, and what is required of the teacher herself.

She then describes how Body Ego Technique is used with infants, preschool children and older children; with adults and with the mentally handicapped, mentally ill, deaf and culturally deprived. There are special chapters on teacher training and sample classes for different ages.

This book gives an extraordinarily vivid depth of specific detail on procedure, materials and technique. But it is more than a manual of technique. Mrs. Salkin illustrates how the teacher must become aware and sensitive to the personal needs of the individual and must use these methods adaptively and with variation. I would add that, hopefully, mastery of technique should leave the teacher free to intervene flexibly and with intuitive understanding.

In 1958, when I first became involved in this area, I was impressed by the potential promise of this work in the area of my own particular research interest—the understanding and treatment of schizophrenic patients. One of our ventures was a controlled scientific study of the use of Body Ego Technique with very regressed chronic patients. In this first trial, the therapists felt that they could establish contact and elicit cooperation in a high proportion of cases. Those treated with Body Ego Technique did significantly better than untreated comparison patients, in terms of overall improvement, affective contact, motility and general functioning.

Unfortunately, we were not able to provide systematic observation of the treatment process. However, informal clinical observation by nonparticipant observers suggested that in some patients improvement occurred that was also manifested in ward behavior, while in other patients there was therapeutic progress in treatment sessions that was not transferred to the ward situation. Some patients, previously mute or uncooperative, reached a point where they were ready and even eager to talk and verbal psychotherapy could be started. Thus our research showed that Body Ego Technique did indeed have potential, not as a magic cure for schizophrenia, but in making contact and establishing a relationship and as an adjunct to, or in preparing the way for other forms of therapy such as psychotherapy and the social therapies.

Now, ten years later, I can see two other, additional, potentials in this approach that I did not perceive then. We talk a lot about prevention, about doing something to prevent mental illness. If our psychodynamic theorizing is correct, that body image and body ego are of central importance both in normal development and in pathological aberration, then systematic attempts to foster its normal development might perhaps have a general value and a legitimate place in our educational system as a preventive measure, as part of our continuing campaign against psychiatric disorders. And, now that it is possible to identify at least some of those who fall in the high risk group for schizophrenia (such as the children of schizophrenic parents), I would strongly advocate special efforts in this direction for these particular children, starting if possible even before nursery school. I would hope that Jeri Salkin's work and this volume will lead to the development and adoption of such training classes and that it will encourage others to do serious research in these areas.

Philip R. A. May, M.D.

Professor of Psychiatry in Residence
Neuropsychiatric Institute
California State Department of Mental Hygiene and
University of California at Los Angeles

Chief of Staff for Program Evaluation, Research and Education
Veterans Administration Hospital
Brentwood, California

BIBLIOGRAPHY

Bellak, L.: The treatment of schizophrenia and psychoanalytic theory. *J of Mental Dis,* *131:*39–46, 1960.

Bellak, L. and Loeb, L.: *The Schizophrenic Syndrome,* New York, Grune and Stratton, 1969.

DesLauriers, A.: The psychological experience of reality. In L. Appleby, J. N. Scher and J. Cummings (Eds.), *Chronic Schizophrenia.* Glencoe, Ill., Free Press of Glencoe, 1960, pp. 275–302.

Federn, P.: *Ego Psychology and the Psychoses.* New York, Basic Books, 1952.

Fenichel, O.: *The Psychoanalytic Theory of Neurosis.* W. W. Norton, New York, 1945.

Fisher, S. and Cleveland, S. E.: *Body Image and Personality.* New Jersey, Van Nostrand, 1958.

Freedman, A. M.: Maturation and its relation to the dynamics of childhood schizophrenia. *Am J Orthopsychiatry, 24:*487–491, 1954.

Freeman, T., Cameron, J. L. & McGhie, A.: *Chronic Schizophrenia.* International University Press, New York, 1958.

Freud, S.: *The Ego and the Id.* London, Hogarth Press, 1927, pp. 26–27.

Greenson, R. R.: Panel: Problems of identification. *J Am Psychoanal Assoc, 1:*538–549, 1953.

Hoffer, W.: Development of the Body Ego. *Psychoanal Study Child, 5:*18–23, 1950.

Jacobson, E.: Depersonalization. *J Am Psychoanal Assoc,* 7:581–610. 1959.

Schilder, P.: *The Image and Appearance of the Human Body.* International University Press, New York, 1950.

Scott, R. D.: The psychology of the body image. *Br J Med Psychol, 24:*254–266, 1951.

ACKNOWLEDGMENTS

I AM MOST GRATEFUL for having had the opportunity to have been a member of the Lester Horton Dance Group. Lester Horton's creative skills and compassion have had a lasting influence upon me. What I learned as a staff member and as a professional performer in his group has been and is the basis for the growth and development of my career and of Body Ego Technique.

I am deeply indebted to Philip R. A. May, M.D. for his recognition and support of Body Ego Technique, for his initiative in obtaining a grant from the State of California Department of Mental Hygiene to explore further this technique, for helping me to articulate more clearly the verbal meaning of this nonverbal technique and for reading the manuscript and writing the Introduction to this book.

I wish to express my gratitude to Stuart S. Turkel, M.D. for his supportive direction of the Body Ego Technique research project at Camarillo State Hospital, for his continued interest and support of my work at Cedars-Sinai Medical Center, and for his contribution in giving his comments and reflections on the technique based upon his involvement.

I am also deeply indebted to Susan Cambigue, a devoted friend and associate teacher, for writing and compiling my class techniques and for illustrating them with her delightful line drawings.

For their sensitivity to the visual subtleties of movement and their ability to capture it photographically I wish to thank Ernest E. Reshovsky and Leo Salkin.

I am grateful to Daniel Gordon, a great friend, who took time to read this manuscript and offered helpful criticism and suggestions.

I also wish to thank Ruth Lert for her painstaking editorial assistance.

My appreciation to Mrs. Dee Newton for reading, typing, correcting and preparing several drafts as well as the final manuscript of this book.

I especially thank Margaret Gage, Dr. Hanna Fenichel, my students, my husband and my daughter for their encouragement and for their faith in my ability to complete this book.

I wish to express my appreciation to the following publishers and individuals who granted permission to quote brief excerpts from various books and articles which helped to enrich the contents of this book:

Ausubel, David P., M.D., Ph.D: *Theory and Problems of Child Development.* New York, Grune & Stratton, Inc., 1958.

Gesell, Gesell, and Amatruda,: *Abnormal Psychology and Modern Life.* Chicago, Scott, Foresman and Company, 1956.

Hamlyn, Paul: 'Beginnings,' in *The World of Children*. London, Paul Hamlyn, Ltd., 1966.

Murphy, Lois Barclay: *Preventive Implication of Development in the Preschool Years*. New York, Basic Books, Inc., 1961.

Piers, Maria, Ph.D.: Play and Mastery (bulletin); Reiss-Davis Child Study Center, Spring, 1967.

Shevrin, Howard, Ph.D. and Toussieng, Povl W., M.D.: Conflict over tactile experiences in emotionally disturbed children. *J Am Acad Child Psychiatry*, October, 1962.

Stolz, Lois Meek, Ph.D.: *Our Changing Understanding of Young Childrens' Fears, 1920–1960*. Washington, D.C., National Association for the Education of Young Children, 1964.

Storr, Anthony: 'Reaching Out for the World,' in *The World of Children*. London, Paul Hamlyn Ltd., 1966.

CONTENTS

BODY EGO TECHNIQUE

PART I

CHAPTER 1

THE THEORY OF
BODY EGO TECHNIQUE

BODY EGO TECHNIQUE is a predominantly nonverbal educational method that concentrates on learning and experiencing a variety of goal-directed physical movement patterns. The elements of bodily movement (rhythm, space, force) are used in a very special goal-directed way to facilitate the development of self-identity, body image and ego structure and to bring about changes of experiences that are necessary for ego growth.

Body Ego Technique is described as predominantly a nonverbal technique because the main focus is on movement rather than on what the person says. The body-ego movement and posture changes can be learned by nonverbal imitation, and in the case of very young children, it is recognized that they learn mostly through imitation.

There are many interrelated experiences and stages of development that must be accomplished in order to produce a mature organized self or ego. One must first distinguish a separateness between self and mother. This literal awareness of having a separate body from one's mother is the origin of feeling a sense of personal identity. One must establish a body self and acquire a picture of how one looks in size and shape; how tall, how short, how fat, how thin and how one relates to other people and objects in space. This is body image, closely related to the sense of self-identity. Self-identity could be described as the subjective sense of continuous personal existence. Anthony Storr says:

> There seems little doubt that, at first, the sense of being a continuing person depends upon continuity of care. If for too long, no one is there, the void opens, we are cut off, we exist no longer.[1]

One of the basic objectives in Body Ego Technique is to broaden the range of subjective experiences in order to eventually bring about a balance of emotional experiences within oneself. The movements taught by the instructor of Body Ego Technique allow the student to experience new and broader subjective changes. For example, if the intention of the teacher is to create the feeling of excitement or nervousness, with or without verbal communication, the movements taught would be small in size and fast in tempo, with an exaggerated amount of tension. The objective would be to

---

[1] Anthony Storr, 'Reaching Out for the World,' in *The World of Children* (London, Paul Hamlyn Ltd.), p. 18, 1966.

try to move at a very fast tempo which would cause the movements to become small and in order to accomplish this speed and size of movement, an exaggerated amount of tension is needed. When this objective is fulfilled, the resultant subjective experience could be one of excitement or nervousness.

Body movement has been used in various ways as an educational and therapeutic tool for the normal developing child, as well as for the physically handicapped, the blind, the deaf, the mentally retarded and the educationally handicapped. Movement is now being used successfully for older individuals as well. Movement has been used as recreational therapy and it is also used in many forms of music, art, dance and psychodrama therapies. The objective in recreational therapy and in some education is usually to accomplish and perfect the skills needed to compete in various forms of activity. Music, art, dance and psychodrama, when not professionally or educationally oriented, usually concentrate on expression and catharsis. Catharsis is the purging of emotions and does not necessarily relate to adaptive behavior—physical and emotional catharsis do not in themselves lead to the maturation of the ego. In Body Ego Technique, an important objective is to interrupt catharsis, when and if it occurs, and at that point to teach the individual goal-directed ways of moving, thus creating a change of experience that helps to bring about ego growth. There are times when it might seem that a prolonged catharsis might be necessary or beneficial. However, it is important to recognize that release of tension per se will not lead towards ego growth.

Catharsis is used in a very special way in Body Ego Technique. It is used in perhaps a broader or more complete sense and it takes on more importance than usual. According to a comprehensive dictionary of psychological and psychoanalytical terms by English and English.[2]

> The esthetic meaning of catharsis is the purification or the purging of emotions by art—Aristotle's original statement was ambiguous and led to two interpretations; that emotional tensions are lessened by expressing them in esthetic experience; or they are refined by sharing in emotions universalized and artistically portrayed.

In Body Ego Technique, catharsis is dealt with in a controlled way—and has a beginning, a middle, and an end. The reason for separating catharsis into a beginning, middle, and end is that each part is important in a different way. In the beginning the teacher or therapist must, through personal encouragement or nonverbal communication, stimulate the student to begin to express a real or imagined experience. Often it is necessary to encourage the young developing child to explore, to try, to take a chance. It may be necessary for the instructor to enter into the student's fixated or routine way of moving in order to stimulate a change of expression. When this change of expression takes place, the student is beginning an emo-

---

[2] Horace B. English and Ava C. English: *A Comprehensive Dictionary of Psychological and Psychoanalytical Terms*. A Guide to Usage. 1st Ed. New York. Longmans, Green, p. 77, 1958.

tional and physical action that could reach an uncontrollable stage. It is impossible for anyone, even the person involved, to know at exactly what point in this expressive act emotional and movement involvement will take over and make it impossible for one to interrupt or stop the action.

The instructor must be very sensitive to the various degrees of external movement patterns expressing emotional motivations. She must know how to encourage a beginning and how to sense the middle before it has started into the end. For instance, a hyperactive or disturbed child can be so easily stimulated and lose control so quickly that the beginning and middle and end are very close together. An old or frightened individual might take a much longer time to be stimulated into any expressive action and may never go beyond the beginning stage.

The middle stage is the most important. Its range varies with each individual and with each emotional expression. It is the stage when the instructor must redirect the action into a change. For instance, when a student has been stimulated by the stamping of the feet and throwing of the arms to begin to express anger, just before he loses control, he can be redirected into other ways of feeling and expressing himself. If, however, the angry expression reaches a point of no control, then a catharsis may progress uncontrollably to physical and emotional exhaustion. In this situation it is literally impossible, at least at that time, to encourage any further action.

The average normal adult limits his range of expression to such a degree that catharsis is seldom experienced even in the theater or on the analytic couch.

The young child often experiences catharsis through his temper tantrums.

In Body Ego Technique catharsis is divided into three separate stages: (1) the beginning—to try to encourage or stimulate movements that will express conscious and unconscious thoughts and feelings; (2) the middle—to allow and encourage physical and emotional expression within the broadest range that the individual seems to be able to control and at some point during this stage, to direct the student through movement into changes of feelings and actions that can lead towards ego growth; (3) the end—to protect the student, through safe environment and understanding, so as to encourage further but different attempts at expressing himself.

In the normal developmental process of ego growth, when there are few physical or emotional interferences, the necessary changes occur as one resolves a problem, passes through a developmental stage, makes a decision or accomplishes a given task in a reality situation. However, during these growth changes, abnormal inhibitions, the fear of having an expression not accepted, or the fear of causing inappropriate or unbalanced reactions can make it difficult, if not impossible, for many individuals to make these needed changes without some guidance. These changes can be especially difficult when they are dependent upon dealing with or responding to ver-

bal expressions whose connotations may have been associated, at one time
or another, with some particular conflict for the person involved; indeed,
a person may be unaware that his external posture or movements may be
related to an unconsciously motivated conflict. It should be noted that although Body Ego Technique deals with the external bodily expressions of
conflict, it can be effective without dealing with a particular conflict on a
conscious level. For instance, the teacher need not label the fast, small,
tense movements as nervousness, nor be concerned about the reality related cause or motivation that the student might be experiencing—just trying to move this way offers much stimulation and security to the individual.

In the application of Body Ego Technique, it is assumed that the total
ego which is the physical body and psychological self is a unity and that
movement and posture are the externalization of the self. What one *feels*
and *is* internally shows and can be seen in some manner of posture or external movement pattern; all movement has meaning and motivation, regardless of whether it is consciously or unconsciously directed.

Developmentally speaking, each person is the product of all of his real
and imagined experiences and of the way in which he has coped with these
experiences—some residue of each experience remains as a part of his conscious or unconscious being. When an unresolved experience manifests itself for a sufficient period of time in the external bodily posture, the body
may undergo physical changes to compensate for this posture. For example,
if a prolonged unresolved experience of fear caused raised shoulders and
a withdrawn neck, this could eventually cause the neck and shoulder
muscles to shorten and therefore have an effect upon the body structure.

The most basic movements of life that can be seen and felt are the puls-
ing heartbeat and the rhythmic flow of the breath. Even these small subtle
movements have force, use space, and have their own individual rhythm.

When the timing, the speed of the rhythm or the amount of force or
space used is varied or changed, then the person feels a variation or change
of experience. When one sits or stands rocking from side to side, the space
used is limited, the rhythm of the breath is even and slow and the force is
repetitious. The resultant experience would undoubtedly be limited and mo-
notonous. If one should run for any distance, the force is greatly increased,
the rhythm of the breath is quickened, the space used is broadened and
these changes cause one to feel differently.

In the use of Body Ego Technique, the approach of the instructor is to
try deliberately to create an external bodily change by teaching changes of
posture, movement patterns, rhythm and tempo, space and force. It is assumed that influencing or changing an individual's physical posture or
movement patterns will also bring about psychological changes.

Movement is also an avenue for affective and instinctual discharge.
Under circumstances that are clearly defined, such as a controlled class environment, these changes of affect are relatively safe psychologically. A
controlled class environment allows, accepts and encourages a person to

experience change of affect without being involved in the type of life experience situation that would usually cause this change. In other words, by learning and carrying out external movement patterns related to different ways of feeling, a reality situation may be simulated, created or recreated.

In many instances, the ways of feeling are experienced one way internally while their external expression is consciously or unconsciously curtailed. The instructor of Body Ego Technique must also be able to see this external curtailment, know the associated internal effect and the possible origin of the emotional motivation. For instance, when one is smiling it usually means that he is happy, pleased or feeling at ease. The muscles around the mouth are flexible and relaxed. Exaggerated muscle tension and a rigid mouth position can produce a false smile. The conscious intention can be to externally express happiness but exaggerated muscle tension and an inflexible smile are incongruous to a happy feeling and could mean that the internal motivation has a different emotional content.

In Body Ego Technique, the movement communication makes it possible to teach, even when all verbal communication has stopped, or has never developed. Nonverbal communication may take place through, for example, direct eye contact, the gentle touch of a hand or a facial expression that says, "I care." For the blind, body manipulation by touch must be reassuring before words can be listened to. For the deaf there are no words so their eyes must listen and learn. And for the crippled, the old, and the autistic children who are functioning in their own world, it may be far more meaningful to touch, feel, see and to move than to listen, hear and do.

But, in most instances, Body Ego Technique can also make use of verbal communication. Although the main form remains essentially nonverbal, the psychotic, the neurotic, the emotionally disturbed, as well as the more balanced individual, can also be reached through the teacher's verbal directions. However, even when the teacher gives verbal directions, she continues, in most instances, to demonstrate the movements. Thus the students or patients themselves never have to verbalize in order to fully participate in a Body Ego Technique class. Silent motivation, connotation, perception and cognizance can be experienced when one moves; however, the understanding and utilization of verbal directions and responses can enrich this experience.

To help broaden the range of subjective experiences and eventually bring about a balance of emotional experiences within oneself, it is also necessary to broaden the physical range of movement. For instance, one can learn to be aware of the various body parts by touching and moving each part separately. As this action takes place, the related words can be used by either student or instructor or both. The physical and muscular structure can be lengthened and strengthened through contractions and stretches. Contract means to shorten and stretch means to lengthen. The body boundaries and spacial awareness can be extended or broadened by moving in and through space, and varying the amount of force, by changing rhythmic structure and the motivation for moving. This concept will be handled in more detail in a later chapter.

In some areas and at some times, the Body Ego Technique instructor may make use of the form of the performing art of dance. The basic difference between movement used for normal everyday communication and the same movement used as dance is the structure, the form and the organized rhythmic repetitions. The rhythmic repetitious movement patterns in dance constitute "drill technique" and are designed to help the dancer gain strength, endurance, flexibility, muscle tone and kinesthetic learning. The objective of "drill technique" for the dancer is to increase his ability to fulfill and enrich his form of communication with his audience. In Body Ego Technique, the rhythmic form is used as a process of learning. This rhythmic repetition is a satisfying way of learning and helps to establish a feeling of organization and accomplishment. This accomplishment, through Body Ego Technique education and therapy, is similar to the use that a child makes of his repetitive play to gain mastery over his environment and his feelings, as well as gaining recognition of self, body image and ego boundaries.

Another important relationship between Body Ego Technique, child's play, and dance is the purposeful make-believe quality. We all make believe as children. A child between the ages of two to six years passes back and forth between reality and make-believe often and with the greatest of ease. After six years, this vacillation becomes less frequent and the child functions more and more in a reality world. As adults we limit the amount of fantasy in which we allow ourselves to become involved.

An artist, such as a dancer, again, freely calls upon the fantasy world for his creative material—in the service of the ego. The mentally ill patient also functions much more freely, back and forth, between fantasy and reality—but in this case, it is not in the service of the ego. In Body Ego Technique, the instructor may deliberately utilize this make believe quality to stimulate the exploration of a wide range of experiences and to help clarify the difference between reality and fantasy.

Regardless of how limited or expansive the subjective physical expression might be, this make-believe type of activity helps to relieve the person involved of the total responsibility for his physical acts and the associated subjective experience. He can always pretend that someone else caused the experience to happen; he did not really mean it or it was only make-believe. These experiences are not recorded and need not be communicated to anyone else.

The contrast between dance and Body Ego Technique appears also in other areas. A performing dancer has to communicate to an audience specific ideas and roles through movement. This is why a dancer must train his physical body to be able to say and feel at any given time, in an abstract form, what he intends to convey rather than to be limited to the reality content of whatever it is that he is experiencing before and during his performance. Even this abstract objective form of communication being performed by a highly trained individual is limited to the subjective possibilities of that individual dancer.

A dancer learns to see, feel, duplicate and abstract into symbolic form movements that are related to the intended portrayal of the character which he is trying to communicate to the audience. He must fulfill the movement to the point of feeling the related emotion in order to gain the empathy of his audience.

In Body Ego Technique, the instructor has a similar task and may use similar methods. She must know the movement patterns that are related to certain emotional feelings. The instructor can learn these related feelings and movement patterns by watching young expressive children and other uninhibited individuals. Having the ability to see and closely duplicate a person's posture and movement patterns allows the instructor to experience, in her own way, a feeling similar to that experienced by the person being observed. In Body Ego Technique, this ability to *see* movement is especially important. It makes the instructor more aware of the student's level of ego functioning, of his stage of development and of his range of physical and emotional experience. Such awareness can provide a starting point in teaching one how to vary, broaden and change his experiences. It is especially important, whether teaching a child or an adult, healthy or sick, to be able to know where they are physically and emotionally and to start at that point to help broaden their education and growth.

Again, like the dancer, the Body Ego Technique instructor must have an extended knowledge of the origins and connotations of movement. In other words, what are the many reasons and combinations of reasons that might cause one to move in a particular way? The instructor must also have a knowledge of the possible variations, extensions and developments of movement patterns, such as what is the logical development of a rocking movement, a walk, a swinging movement. What is an opposition or contrast to a given movement? When is it better to teach an extreme contrast in movement and when is it better to gradually develop the movement? To know all of this, the instructor must know the broad range of meanings or connotations that all movements have.

The purpose of this book is to try to cover these materials and help the teacher to understand how to utilize the elements of movement (rhythm, space, force) in a variety of ways to help educate, reeducate and to facilitate the development of self-identity, body image and ego strength.

CHAPTER 2

THE RELATIONSHIP OF BODY EGO TECHNIQUE TO EARLY CHILDHOOD DEVELOPMENT

THE SPECIFIC OBJECTIVES of Body Ego Technique are closely related to the normal developmental stages that a child passes through during the first five years of life. The content of the sessions deals with variations of rhythm, timing, space, distance, quality, affect and force, and with separateness, body awareness, self and object relationship, body boundaries, limitations, creativeness and role playing. Each developmental stage, starting with the first sign of life—a lusty cry when a new born baby begins to breathe—deals with, in one way or another, these same materials.

It has been recognized by child development authorities that the experience a child has during the first five years of life and the way in which he copes with these experiences can, in part, remain with him and influence his actions throughout his lifetime.

In its mother's womb the development of its eyes, hands and brain has miraculously re-traced the course of their evolution in the entire human species—from the fish of 400 million years ago that first acquired eyes, from the preprimates of fifty million years ago that first learned to manipulate their hands.

Perhaps because of this slowly acquired complexity, human babies, after birth, are the slowest earthly creatures to reach growth. A human child takes over twenty years to mature, and during most of that time it needs protection not required by any other animal. Today, psychologists, neurologists and biologists are busy trying to assess babies' brains and bodies, as well as their consciousness. Science has brought us much new knowledge so that today, as never before, the importance of a child's experiences in his beginnings is generally appreciated, if not fully understood.

To be conscious of where one's body begins and ends is such an achievement that, even years afterwards, in fever and in dreams, the demarcation line between self and world can sometimes become blurred again. During illness, for example, many people can remember that they have experienced a kind of distortion of the image of their body, so that a thumb or the tongue seems disproportionately enormous. Often the perception of both time and space also becomes altered in illness, so that at such moments an adult may recapture what we imagine must be the infant's experience before order has been imposed upon the world, or time conceived as measurable duration.[3]

---

[3] Paul Hamlyn, 'Beginnings,' in *The World of Children* (London, Paul Hamlyn, Ltd.), pp. 15–17, 1966.

Body Ego Technique strives to help the child through the process of learning, the order his world imposes on him and to help him to conceive of time as measurable duration, as well as to establish a clear body image.

Lois Barclay Murphy, in an article, *Preventive Implications in the Preschool Years* says,

> In a child, physical illness and emotional disturbances threaten to, or actually do interfere with the process of growth itself . . . We want to look at both the factors that contribute to the child's resources for coping with everyday stress and with crisis, and his capacity to maintain internal integration: that is, to continue to make developmental progress with an adequate degree of mental health. The more we understand these, the better foundation we will have for prevention work. . . . Disturbances arise either from too little or too much, too soon or too late, in relation to the needs or demands, limits, and tempo of the individual child. . . . We also deal with both inner and external factors in the maintenance of integration: factors that need to be appreciated if prevention is to be effective. . . . we often find that individual stressful experiences have come too fast or frequently for the child to integrate or absorb one before he is bowled over by the next; or the child has lacked the support he needed for his own spontaneous ways of coping with stress; or the stresses occurred at a critical phase when an important new function such as speech or locomotion was emerging. The incompletely established new functions are then vulnerable to stress and insecurity. . . . in all cases the central problem becomes (within himself and in his relations to the environment) the question of the extent of the child's resources for coping with stress in such a way as to permit growth, increasing integration, confidence, and mutually gratifying exchanges between and interactions with his environment. When he cannot handle stress, that is when he is overwhelmed—immobilized, made panicky, frantic, blocked—he needs active assistance and support for his efforts to achieve better integration, and to grow.

> The problem of prevention, then, is one of assessing the external and internal factors in the child's experience of stress and crisis and the child's capacities to deal with it; then finding ways to support the child's efforts toward mastery. This can include both medical, social and psychologic help (giving him usable knowledge and insight where he can use it, as before an operation; comfort in the terms that can help him; support for mastery in his terms; compensatory gratifications that have value for him; opportunities for discharge of tension; help in communicating his experience of stress; doses of challenge, reality testing, and stimulus to give up unconstructive defenses at a pace he can manage; appreciation of his efforts to cope and progress in coping). This can go parallel to management of the environment to prevent the child from becoming overwhelmed by stress with which he cannot cope.[4]

The method used in teaching Body Ego Technique is designed to: (a) facilitate the development of the ego and self-identity in the normal child; (b) help prevent an inability to cope with stress and crisis by giving him support for mastery in his own terms; (c) give him the opportunity for discharge of tension; (d) help him to communicate his experience of stress;

[4] Lois Barclay Murphy, "Preventive Implications in the Preschool Years," excerpted from chapter 10, in *Prevention of Mental Disorders in Childhood*, edited by Gerald Caplan, © 1961, (New York, Basic Books, Inc.) Based on findings from The Coping Project, supported by The Menninger Foundation and U.S.P.H.S. Grant M-680, pp. 218, 223, 227.

(e) give him doses of challenge, reality testing and stimulus to give up unconstructive defenses at a pace he can manage.

> As a result of their intensive studies of thousands of infants and children, Gesell and Gesell-and-Amatruda have shown that human development tends to follow a definite schedule, not only in physical and motor development, but also in emotional, intellectual and social development. The infant crawls and sits up before he begins to walk, his language behavior progresses from random vocalizing to words that eventually become vehicles for thinking. Of course, this entire sequence of events is dependent upon and influenced by the surrounding environment. Disease, injury, privation, or other adverse conditioning may interfere with normal development, particularly during early life. Environmental factors which interfere with the normal scheduling of growth processes are likely to have serious consequences—at each stage certain specific tasks are imposed upon the individual by maturational or social pressures or both, which he must master if he is to maintain a normal course of development. If these various tasks are not mastered during the appropriate developmental period, the individual will suffer from immaturities and incompetencies which will carry over and handicap his adjustment in later developmental levels. . . . it is possible for development to be arrested or fixated at different points along the continuum from infancy to maturity, or the developmental sequence may be reversed, as in regression, where the individual reverts to behavior which once brought satisfaction.[5]

The progression of the developmental stages, as well as regression, are recognizable in behavior and are externalized in posture and movement.

Here again, Body Ego Technique, with its specific objectives, deals directly and indirectly with the education of the developing young child, as well as helping him to overcome or correct the immaturities and incompetencies which could have been caused by an inappropriate developmental sequence.

Experts in the study of human development tend to agree that physical, motor, emotional, intellectual and social development follow a rather definite schedule during the first five years of life. However, regardless of how simple, normal or definite this early developmental pattern seems to be, no one thinks that it is easily accomplished. No one thinks it is accomplished without stress and crisis. Each individual can benefit from some active assistance along the way.

Each individual must develop a body image, a self-identity and ego structure. Body Ego Technique uses body movement to aid in the development of a body image, a self-identity and ego structure.

> Since the child's world begins inevitably with the body, and since the force which instigates the child to expand his knowledge is always the pressure of bodily desires, and since every new fact of experience which enters into psychic life can make its entrance only by relating itself to that which is already present,

---

[5] James C. Coleman, *Abnormal Psychology and Modern Life* (Chicago, Scott, Foresman and Company, 1956).

it follows that every new fact apperceived by the child must somehow relate itself to bodily things.[6]

The theory of Body Ego Technique recognizes that the psychic life and the physiological body are one; therefore, not only does every new fact apperceived by a child relate to bodily things, but also the physical posture and movements are the externalization of the internal psychic experience. This total body is the visible reality of that life.

All children under the age of five pass through the struggle of the early developmental stage; all children over the age of five, as well as all adults, function with a greater or lesser residue of these accomplished or unaccomplished early developmental patterns. Many older children and adults function with various levels of fixated immaturities and incompetencies. Many others regress to the level of a developmental stage which perhaps offers more comfort or security.

The instructor of Body Ego Technique recognizes the importance of having a clear knowledge of the normal developmental patterns and of the chronological sequence in which they are accomplished. This knowledge and the ability to see movement and to separate the elements of movement allow the instructor to be objective and to know at what level to teach the student those changes of experience that are necessary for ego growth.

The development that takes place during the first year of life seems to exceed that which occurs in any other such period of time. The lungs are inflated to start the rhythmic breath and create the first birth cry. The generalized activity that accompanies the cry seems to be involuntary and random at first but is seemingly gradually related to a deliberate purpose. Muscle strength and dexterity seem to start at the top of the body and move towards the feet. The baby turns his head when lying down and soon he can hold up his chin. By the age of nine weeks he can raise both the head and the chest from a prone position.

Each child is born with and seems to maintain a characteristic rhythm of breathing, sucking and swallowing. The baby makes sounds, follows movement with his eyes and seems to hear sound. He moves from side to side, grasps objects and reaches. His eyes and mouth still seem to be his most active muscles. He looks at his own hand and begins to observe others. He rolls over and sits up, first with support and then without any support. This usually takes place between six and eight months of age.

Many other steps are being accomplished around this time of development. The child can pick up objects, transfer them from one hand to the other, and he reacts to his own image in the mirror. He reaches, pulls himself up, begins to gain eye-hand coordination and some spatial awareness. He begins to make choices and reacts to the tone and rhythm of voices around him. He can coordinate most of the large muscles and some of the small ones. He crawls and creeps to reach his intended goal. He pushes and

---

[6] Lawrence K. Kubie, "The physical basis of personality," *Child Study*, Vol. 11, pp. 131–160, 1934.

pulls toys, throws objects and is able to pick them up again. He climbs, he catches and he builds. He stands alone, walks holding on to support, and then walks alone. When a child first walks, he elevates the arms over head and spreads the legs rather far apart. These two positions are to help balance the newly uprighted body.

> The young infant can only cry and thrash about; the young child can hide, run away, strike out, shout defiance or argue contentiously. Later, culturally directed training further restricts the range of acceptable alternatives and specifies the appropriate type of response and the time, place and conditions under which it may be legitimately made. In our culture, lower-class children learn to express their emotions in motor activity, middle-class children, on the other hand, are taught to express their feelings in more abstract and ideational form. In all children a tendency toward more subtle, symbolic and devious affective expression is a regular accompaniment of emotional development. But despite selectively greater utilization of covert expressive components, the correspondence between two kinds of reactions tends to improve with increasing age, indicating a more integrated type of total organismic response.
>
> Invariably, as children grow older, the culture demands greater suppression of overt emotionality, and accordingly the former gradually learn increased emotional control.[7]

The young infant, the young child and even the adult seem to struggle constantly to find a balance of appropriate affect in their emotional and physical expression. It always seems to be too much or too little or at the wrong time.

After the first year, during which most children learn to stand, fall, squat, walk and turn, the run begins to develop. The second year brings greater skill in walking and running, not only forward, but backward and in circles. The two-year-old also begins to gallop, jump and turn in locomotion. Most children are at least three years old before they can hop or skip. In the Body Ego Technique sessions with preschoolers, the average age for developing the skip is between three and four years of age. Some two-year-olds accomplish this important feat, but sometimes a child is five or six years old before he can coordinate the step and hop that make up the skip.

> The motor ability of a child constitutes an important component of his feeling of competence in coping with the environment. . . . Motor activity is an important outlet for emotional expressions (fear, flight, rage, aggression) and source of basic satisfactions and self-expression. Increased motor competence helps reduce frustrations in childhood that are occasioned by inability to manipulate objects and play materials as desired. The way in which a child expresses himself in motor performance is also an excellent reflection of such temperamental and personality characteristics as venturesomeness, energy level, aggressiveness, sociality, and self confidence.[8]

---

[7] David P. Ausubel, *Theory and Problems of Child Development* (New York, Grune & Stratton, Inc.), pp. 322–323, 1958.

[8] *Ibid.*, p. 509.

The body then (the infant's or his mother's—it matters not to the baby) can be considered the first toy.

The child discovers how to make blocks go through openings, to pull the fire engine on wheels, to fill and empty the pitcher, to scribble with a crayon on paper. He fills and pulls and fits and scribbles, and the fun is more and more in the doing. That a two-year-old's play, with its emphasis on action, its trials and errors, its repetition, is really learning, is self-evident. And, gradually, the child begins to enjoy what he has achieved. Not the filling but the full pitcher. Not the fitting of the blocks into the opening, but the fact that they actually land on the bottom of the box, not the scribbling per se, but the finished page, adorned perhaps with three or four circular configurations.

By the time a child enters nursery school, the main fun lies clearly not in the doing anymore, but in the completed task. His actions are governed not so much by the primitive FUNKTIONSLUST, but to a much larger extent by the instinct to master.

It isn't always easy for adults to keep up with a young child's developmental changes. The switch from bodily sensations to the doing, to the achieving, sometimes escapes our attention. Thus, some of us keep foisting finger paints, sand and clay on the preschool child, marvelling at his gloriously free expression as he obligingly regresses. . . . Every preschooler is under the sway of strong impulses of love and hate and is in conflict about both. Every preschooler is also filled with a drive toward mastery which, in the long run, accrues to actual coping. All the elements of future coping techniques seems to be present in the preschool child's play. All the modes of learning are clearly distinguishable and pure, not, as in later years, in an admixture. . . .

The repetition of a gratifying experience and the assimilation of anxiety are regarded by some experts as the central functions of play. In addition, we would venture to say that play can also be a pure manifestation of the drive toward mastery. This seems particularly clear during the oedipal phase, when a child is usually in nursery school. As he plays, insight learning and identification each appear in unmixed purity leading toward mastery of the inner and the outer world. The behavior of the human race is not merely motivated by id impulses and defences against them, but also by a strong urge toward mastery. Preschool play is its manifestation par excellence.[9]

In Body Ego Technique, the instructor can recognize and help overcome developmental lags in the normal child. Not only must the instructor see if the child can crawl, walk, run, turn, gallop, hop and skip, but in what way does he perform these locomotor movements. How much space does he use? How does he relate in space to himself as well as to other objects? Does he use appropriate affect when he moves? Does it seem, from his posture and movement, that he is arrested or fixated at some earlier developmental stage? Can he make-believe, pretend, and can he play?

. . . Children who cannot play as an outlet, often seem "cranky" and exhibit behavior problems, returning to infantile modes of behavior, such as bed-wetting,

---

[9] Maria Piers, Play and Mastery (bulletin of Reiss-Davis Child Study Center,) Spring, 1967.

thumb-sucking, demands for affection, temper tantrums, withdrawal of emotional interest from adults. . . .[10]

The entire area of mental illness in a child has to be looked at in developmental terms; how does this reaction to stress or crisis affect the motor, cognitive, affective integrations that are of special importance to a child of this age, and to a child of this temperamental style? For this reason, workers with children need a thorough knowledge of developmental processes and sequences, and also the wide range of individual differences within an overall outline of developmental sequences through which children move in the process of growing up. . . .[11]

The many quotations in this chapter have been used to emphasize the importance placed upon the early developmental processes. The objective seems to be the same, whether helping a healthy normal child find his strengths and security, unblocking or easing the strain of the disturbed child or helping an individual overcome immaturities and incompetencies or regressions to this early developmental sequence.

How these objectives are attempted and accomplished in Body Ego Technique will be the content of the following chapters of this book. The material will point out how similar these objectives can be as well as what the subtle or obvious differences might be in working with the normal, the blind, the deaf and with the mentally ill, whether child or adult.

---

[10] Lois Meek Stolz, *Our Changing Understanding of Young Childrens' Fears, 1920–1960* (National Association for the Education of Young Children, 1964), p. 17.

[11] Murphy, "Preventive Implication of Development in the Preschool Years," p. 219.

CHAPTER 3

MOVEMENT: FORCE, SPACE AND RHYTHM

THERE IS NOTHING MYSTERIOUS or unreal about movement. Movement does not just happen. Movement must be motivated, created, executed and it is, consciously or unconsciously, controlled by the individual moving. This is the basis of Body Ego Technique and is perhaps the most distinguishing feature of the way in which movement with its various elements is used in Body Ego Technique in contrast to the way it is used in dance therapies and interpretative and expressive dance classes, sensitivity, encounter and happening groups, all of which usually concentrate on abstract form, expression or catharsis.

Movement is force using space with rhythm. In other words, all movement, which is inherent to all life, is made up of various degrees of force moving in or through space at a given rate of speed or time.

The rate of the movement is the tempo of the rhythm used. The rhythm is the flow of the force with pulsations such as rise and fall, contract and release, beginning and end or a repetitious action caused by a renewed accent.

Accent is a stronger, larger or sharper value, emphasizing a repetitious beginning of a rhythmic measure or phrase of movement.

A measure is exactly that. It is a group of pulses or movements measured and repeated as indicated by the accented beginning.

A phrase is a group of measures or patterns similar to the statements or thoughts of a sentence or a paragraph. They relate to each other.

Space is the area in which movement takes place. One may move *in* space which is called axial space, or one may move *through* space which is called locomotor space.

If one moves around one's own body, vertically, horizontally, diagonally or circularly, he is moving in axial space. Such movements include breathing, reaching, turning in place, moving separate parts of the body like the head, the shoulders, arms, chest, hips, legs, or clapping the hands.

When one moves from one spot to another spot covering a floor pattern of directions such as forward, backward, sideways circularly or diagonally, one is using locomotor space. The movements used to progress from one place to another are called locomotor skills.

Awareness of one's body image allows one to perform locomotor skills with a clear relationship to other objects. Locomotor skills require the development of muscle strength, coordination, flexibility, timing, endurance, dexterity and balance. These are teaching objectives of Body Ego Technique. Locomotor movement skills are rolling, crawling, creeping, walking, running, galloping, sliding, turning, jumping, hopping, leaping and skipping.

Turning, jumping and hopping can be performed while remaining in one place and so may also be considered axial space movement skills.

Rolling is the movement that develops after a baby can turn from front to back or from prone to supine positions. A baby can continue the turn when the momentum of the entire body weight causes a repetitious turn in the same direction. This continuous turn in one direction is a roll.

The crawl is usually motivated by a desire to reach for a distant object. It is the beginning of space orientation. The crawl is a movement that is accomplished by drawing the body along the floor in a prone position with the head and shoulders raised. The arms pull the body forward, and usually the legs and feet help by pushing.

Creeping and crawling are often referred to interchangeably; however, creeping occurs when the locomotion is accomplished by rising to the hands and knees with the trunk or torso free and parallel to the floor.

A turning movement can be axial or locomotor. The axial turn (in place), develops before the locomotor turn because it requires less strength, balance and coordination. A locomotor turn requires balance and the shifting of weight from one foot and leg to the other, with enough strength to carry the entire weight on one foot and leg at a time.

Another axial space movement is the squat, which is to crouch or sit down on the heels with the weight still on the feet. This axial space movement happens often as the baby is struggling and developing enough strength to stand and to walk.

The fall also occurs often at this time of development, dropping from an erect position to the floor, off balance and then gaining equilibrium, over and over again.

A walk is a progressive movement, advancing forward and later backward, as well as in a variety of floor patterns. Floor pattern is the pattern or design that one makes on the floor as he moves in and through space. The movement of a walk is lifting one leg and foot off the floor, placing it in front of the other leg and foot, alternately shifting the weight onto the advancing leg and foot. Both feet are never off the ground at the same time. The arms swing in opposition for balance.

A run is the same kind of locomotor movement as the walk, with the same kind of foot and arm alternation, but it is performed at a faster tempo or pace.

A gallop, as used in Body Ego Technique, is a forward progression in which one foot remains in front of the other and locomotion is accomplished by lifting the front foot and stepping forward while lifting or dragging the back foot up to the front one. The child first gallops by keeping one or the other foot on the ground, supporting the weight at all times.

The slide is the same movement as the gallop. However, the body turns sideways, and the gallop progresses sideways, changing it into a slide.

A jump occurs when both feet leave the floor at the same time and return to the floor at the same time. This skill requires enough muscular development and strength to lift the entire weight of the body off the floor at the same time.

A hop is much more difficult than a jump, because the entire body weight is on one foot and leg while the other foot is held in the air. One leg and foot lift the weight, leave the floor, return to the floor, and this movement is repeated without ever taking weight on the foot held in the air. One can progress by hopping through space or one can hop in place.

A leap occurs when one takes off from the floor on one leg and foot, followed by the other leg and foot. As both legs and feet progress through the air, off the floor at the same time, the back leg passes the front leg and one lands on the floor on the opposite foot and leg from which he took off from the floor. A leap is similar to a broad run. The weight shifts from one leg and foot to the other alternately.

The skip is a combination of a step and a hop. This simple combination of movements requires much muscular development, strength, coordination and balance. A skip is the first *combination* of locomotor skills and is the last gross motor developmental skill that a child learns in the first five years of life.

All of the basic large muscle movements are learned during the first five years of life and movement refinement develops after that time. A much greater skill and ability to use the large muscles and to perform these basic movements becomes apparent between the ages of six and eleven years. During this span, eye-hand movement perception is established. By the time a child is eleven years old his proficiency in physical movement skills has developed to an adult level.

All movement has motivation which determines how one moves and the resultant act always includes force, space and rhythm.

Some other terms used to express the element of force are: the amount of energy, the dynamics of movement, type of movement, the style of movement, the way one moves and the reason one moves.

Each type of movement, each style of movement and each different reason that motivates movement determine or change the amount of force (rhythm and space) used to perform that movement.

In Body Ego Technique, the recognized types of movement are: (1) swing movements, (2) staccato, (3) sustained, (4) suspended, (5) percussive, (6) vibratory and (7) relaxed movements.

Swing movement always starts with a dropping or downward action that reaches a suspended point before repeating the drop or downward action through a pendular swing. An example is the alternating arm swing when one is walking or running.

Suspended or extended movement is a movement held in midair or sustained somewhere between top and bottom as when one reaches above one's height.

A sustained movement is a slow continuation of energy, as felt in a slow and even act of pushing.

Staccato movement is jerky and sharp with a stop or short hold between each movement, causing the jerky action. The tempo can be fast or slow.

Percussive movement is a strong, striking, abrupt movement as when beating a drum or pounding with a hammer.

Vibratory movements are repeated, fast percussive actions: back and forth, to and fro. The speed of the movements make them small in size such as quivering, shaking or vibrating.

A relaxed movement is a movement with an equal amount or a balance of tension and release, when standing, sitting, or lying down. A total loss of energy and/or tension causes one to collapse. When a collapse takes place, it may be difficult to guide a person into a different movement or change.

The objective of Body Ego Technique is to use change of movement to help bring about the equivalent goal-directed change in experience. After a collapse one feels drained and relieved and is unable to direct his interest towards growth or change. After the collapse is over, one once again begins to build up tension.

Style of movement as used in dance and Body Ego Technique, usually means ethnic style, such as Spanish, Mexican, Gypsy, African, Hawaiian, etc., or Ballet, Mime, Tap, Modern, Modern Jazz, Contemporary, Interpretive or Creative Modern Dance.

The style of Body Ego Technique originates in the style of creative modern dance, which is attuned to the early childhood developmental movement patterns. Because this form or style of movement is based on the more natural way of moving, it offers the broadest range of movement patterns, as well as the normal externalization of thought processes. The emotional expression, the idea or the story being communicated through the physical action of creative modern dance or of Body Ego Technique is based on real or imaginary situations taken from one's dreams, wishes or reality experiences in life.

The rhythmic part of movement starts with the very first pulse of the breath and continues throughout one's lifetime. Rhythm is the most basic, the most individual and the easiest to see. It is so basic a part of life that most individuals are unaware of their own individual timing. It takes a great deal of training for a person to learn a given rhythm and to function at that learned pace for any amount of time. Pace and tempo are relative and a fast tempo for one individual might be rather slow for another individual. Because rhythm, timing or pace are so obvious and easy to observe, the Body Ego Technique instructor is able to utilize in many ways the variations of rhythmic structure.

> Movement is a universal language. We all use it. We all understand it. Each of us starts life with our own inborn traits and characteristics. Though each individual must do his own growing at his own learning rate, normally we all pass through the same physical developmental pattern.[12]

And these basic developmental patterns are movement, which is made up of rhythm, space and force.

---

[12] *Film, 'Body Ego Technique'* by Salkin-Salkin-Schoop.

CHAPTER 4

TEACHING BODY EGO TECHNIQUE

> Teaching itself is an art. Writing about teaching is an even rarer form of art. For it takes great skill with language to communicate on the printed page, the quality of that subtle and complex transaction which is the core of good teaching.[13]

THAT "SUBTLE AND COMPLEX transaction which is the core of good teaching" is even more subtle and complex when trying to write about movement. Movement must be *experienced*. One does not have that same experience when reading, writing or talking about movement. In order to learn Body Ego Technique, one must understand, be able to see, feel, touch and experience movement. The previous chapters have explained the basic elements of movement and how movement is universally used as an external visible expression in all people of all ages and in different conditions. Therefore, the answer to the question everyone asks, "Where does one find the material to teach?" is that the material is always there, in every form of life.

It is perhaps true that it is almost impossible to teach someone how to be a good teacher; nevertheless, it is possible to teach a good teacher what to teach and how to teach and how to organize the elements of movement in order to accomplish specific goals.

The overall goal of Body Ego Technique, as well as of many other forms of education and therapy, is to help establish a balance of physical and emotional behavior within the individuals involved.

This broad and somewhat overwhelming goal must begin with an aware, objective instructor. In other words, the teacher cannot be trying to balance her subjective behavior while teaching a class in Body Ego Technique.

If you succeed in being objective (which means to be able to view events, ideas, etc. as external and apart from self-consciousness) about what and why you are teaching, you will not become too personally involved or overly sympathetic towards your students.

Adopting this important attitude allows the form (the use of the elements of movement) to be effective within a much broader range than when the relationship and accomplishments are dependent upon personal feelings and reactions.

---

[13] Robert R. Kirsch, Book Report, *Los Angeles Times*, February 6, 1967, Part IV, p. 8.

If the instructor becomes too concerned with the personal feelings and emotional reactions of the student it can lead into a sympathetic involvement. When one sympathizes he shares in the suffering or emotional feelings. He commiserates by entering into the feelings, the interests and the emotional experiences of the student. The instructor cannot be objective when sympathy and pity cause the wrong form of involvement with the student's personal reactions and needs. On the other hand, the instructor must have and use empathy. Empathy means to be accepting, understanding and to apprehend the state of mind of another person without feeling (as in sympathy) what the other feels. While the emphatic process is primarily intellectual, emotion is not precluded, but it is not the same emotion as that of the person with whom one empathizes. The instructor can, for instance, empathize with a student's anger and still be able to stand aside, look at it objectively and help direct him into changes of emotional feelings. If the instructor has sympathy for the student's anger, she will feel the anger right along with him, help him express it, but will not be able to offer any objective guidance or change.

So, you can have empathy, be a warm and personable teacher and still remain objective.

Before going on to the more specific goals of a Body Ego Technique class, let me remind you again that an individual can experience only that which is his to experience. The technique, the goals and the teacher are objective—but the experience is only subjective. You can be a well-balanced teacher only if at that time you are a well-balanced objective individual.

The specific goals of a class are determined by what you plan to accomplish in a single class, a week's time or perhaps a longer period of time. The easiest way to set specific goals is to start with your overall goal, then break that down into more realistic shorter spans of time, and so on, down to what you plan to accomplish within a single session or even part of a session.

Some dancers, choreographers and teachers have a tendency to limit their teaching to the use of the abstract form of movement, such as shape, time, energy, motion, and choose to ignore the basic motivation that causes the variations of these elements. They seem unaware of the basic results in emotional experience that the changes of these various elements create or motivate. Sometimes there is too much verbal explanation. Demonstrating movement is especially important when teaching children, because imitation is their most effective way of learning.

I would like to point out again some of the values of this nonverbal communication. It is not necessary to *talk* about your goals with your class; it is not necessary to *explain* what and how you are teaching; you can *show* them. You do not need to ask for verbal reactions or responses to what you are teaching in order to have your students fully participate in a class; you can see them. When you demonstrate, and your students try to imitate, no one, absolutely no one, can possibly do exactly the same movement with exactly the same feeling or experience, regardless of how well they can imitate. And actual demonstration and imitation is the most effective way to stimulate and teach movement or dance. Every individual is truly unique and his ability to imitate the movements he sees is limited to that individual uniqueness. The teacher of Body Ego Technique must have a broad range of emotional and physical experiences to call upon; she must be able to see, demonstrate and imitate movement patterns related to her own emotional feelings, as well as being able to utilize the many variations the students externalize.

When a class is finished, it is important for you as a teacher to evaluate your lesson. Did you accomplish your goals? How well was your presentation accepted by the class? Could you improve your teaching technique? Could you use more, better or different materials, and, if so, what and why and how?

The general structure of all classes is much the same. The progression of a class depends upon the age, the condition and the amount of experience the average student in the class has had.

All classes should include the following: (1) a warm-up, (2) strength-building drill technique, (3) rhythm, (4) axial-(center floor) space technique, (5) stretches, (6) progressions (locomotor skills), (7) creative work, (8) use of props, (9) organized movement patterns or the accomplishment of a simple dance.

Each of these categories covers a tremendous amount of material with many variations.

To *warm up* literally means to warm the muscles by increasing the blood circulation. When your skin, muscles and tendons are warm, they are softer and more flexible. A cold physical body is not flexible and is therefore unprepared for the exaggerated kinds of movements and speeded-up tempos that are required as the class progresses. A warm-up is relatively unimportant with children, especially very young ones, because their active bodies are almost always in a state of warm flexibility. On the other hand the majority of all others, especially those who do not exercise regularly, are apt to pull or tear a cold unflexible muscle. Dancers' and athletes' injuries, however, most often come from overuse. An overfatigued body is vulnerable to injury.

Strength-building technique means to strengthen the muscles of the feet, the legs, the abdomen, the buttocks, as well as the upper back, arms, hands and chest. With the exception of the abdominal exercises, these strengthening techniques are more easily accomplished by holding onto a rail (called a barre by the dance professionals) or being supported by holding onto the wall, someone's hand or some other object. It eases the problem of trying to hold your balance and allows for more concentration upon the movements you are trying to accomplish.

When I speak of *rhythm*, I am referring to a special section of the class that deals with rhythm as the dominant action, rather than the overall rhythm that is, of course, a part of all movement. This rhythmic section can deal with exaggerated breathing exercises, which if done too long make one very dizzy, or the rhythmic pace of each individual, or by hand clapping, which is one of the most successful ways of teaching rhythm. When possible, especially with children, using drums or rhythm sticks or other small simple percussive instruments seems to add courage and more awareness to the individual's rhythm. Perhaps it relieves the individual of some responsibility because it is an extension of the body.

When the class moves center floor, or uses *axial space*, a new and different kind of responsibility is experienced. One feels responsible for the space around him. He must not be too close to another, nor too far away. He becomes aware of front and back and up and down and side and side and all the way around. He becomes aware of shape and size and distance, not only his own shape and size (body image) but that of those around him. It is interesting how difficult this kind of spacing is before a student has a fairly clear body image.

Stretches mean, of course, that one stretches or extends one's limbs or total body. Stretches should not be attempted before being thoroughly warmed-up. Stretches can be accomplished either at, or on, the barre (or support), or they can more easily be performed while sitting or standing center floor.

Progressions, including simple *locomotor skills*, are movements and combinations of movements that start in one place and end up in another. In a class, progressions are usually performed on a diagonal line across the longest dimension of the room being used. The warm-up, the stretches, the center floor technique, the rhythmic section and the strength-building techniques, all are in preparation for fulfilling the locomotor progressions. Moving through space, as in progressions, is extremely satisfying, whether moving alone, with a partner or in a group.

Creative work includes: the individual way in which you perform a given movement, creatively solving a given problem or suggestion, improvising movements to various sounds, rhythmic patterns or to music, as well as actually making up a story, real or imagined, or communicating creative ideas through movement. Often the creative work or improvisation includes props.

Props can be used to enhance, broaden or sometimes, when needed, to stimulate and teach such things as colors, shapes, qualities and textures. The word prop is used to mean such objects that are separate from the student and can be used as an extension of his movements or can add a different quality to the movement. Props may include scarves of many colors and sizes. Scarves are especially popular with children. It seems that the choice of colors is quite consistent with the individual and it can be very upsetting if their favorite color is not available. The younger children also enjoy passing the scarves to their classmates, probably because they can find their choice of color before giving them to the others. The soft silk texture seems significant to all students and sometimes they are reluctant to return the scarves to the teacher. The smaller scarves can be tied together and they are often used for impromptu costumes. The larger scarves allow two individuals to work together with one scarf. This limitation stimulates creative interesting movements, as well as offering a different kind of relationship with the partner with whom one is working. Rope or large round elastic can be used in a similar way. The scarves have a floating quality when tossed into the air and allowed to float to the floor. The students can try to duplicate this quality with their own bodies.

Fans can be used to establish definite qualities and styles of movement. The feeling of shyness as well as that of dignity reaches a depth that would be very hard to achieve without this added prop. There is always the ethnic quality that adds a very special importance to the use of the fan. With the more advanced students there is a real challenge of hand agility in the opening and closing of the fan while moving.

Large sheets of heavy plastic have been used to help stimulate gross swinging and throwing movements. However, the students with whom it is safe to use plastic seldom seem to need this added prop for stimulation or for learning duplication.

Balls, balloons and various other shaped objects are used to help clarify the shapes such as round, square, triangle, etc. Balls are also used to show the bounce. This particular kind of prop adds very little to the class that is capable of understanding and experiencing, for instance, a bounce with their own feet and legs. It adds nothing but a burden to the class in which the individuals have a distorted body image.

Percussive instruments, such as rhythm sticks, drums or tambourines can be used by the student while moving, carrying the instrument and beating a rhythmic sound.

Often props are used when they are really not necessary and they then can become a burden or distraction rather than a help to the student who is trying to increase his movement knowledge.

The same is true of an overuse of verbal imagery. It is not necessary to use imagery for the sections of a class that deal with the realistic development of the body and body image such as in the warm-up, strength building and stretching movements, nor is it needed in the learning and practicing of skills. Most children, as well as many adults, are somewhat confused at times about the difference between fantasy and reality. Imagery should be used to help clarify the difference.

A student can learn body alignment more easily when he is taught how to realistically adjust his own body rather than to be told to imagine that there is a man up above him, that the student is a puppet and the man is pulling the strings to make him stand straight. The instructor may know what puppets are; that they are lifeless objects being manipulated by a harmless man, and that most people enjoy watching them. But the student may not want to feel that a stranger is manipulating his body or that he must identify with a lifeless object, or he may have been frightened by a puppet show. By the time the burden of the unnecessary imagery has been dealt with, the good posture or body alignment has been lost. Most students have a rather active imagination and imagery can best be used to stimulate the fantasy than can be expressed in movement. *The safest and most effective way to use imagery is to elicit the ideas from your students.* They can handle much greater horror or drama if the suggestion has come from them rather than the instructor. Young children enjoy pretending to be animals. Let them choose the one that may hold a challenge for them, or that perhaps they are especially fond of. It is wise to emphasize the fantasy or *pretend* aspect of the imagination and the acting out of it rather than the *being* of something unreal. The *pretend* attitude allows for a clearer feeling of self reality and purposeful fantasy.

A child is at least six years old before he can begin to clearly distinguish between fact and fantasy, and he is much older before it is really clear to him that he can exhibit some controls.

In any class there is a great need for the feeling of accomplishment, or an ending or a temporary completion. Especially with children or non-dancers, it is important to finish a class with a simple structured, learned combination of movements. For example: Form a circle—skip in four times, skip back out four times. Repeat—and then the whole group in a circle formation slides right eight times, left eight times and repeat—each individual then turns right for eight counts and left for eight counts and ends the dance with a bow or curtsey. Children can also add a curtsey or bow, or some other recognition to the teacher, the accompanist and their classmates. This is the beginning of learning how a performing artist, nonverbally says, "Thank you," and shows respect for the help he has received from his fellow humans.

An important attribute of good teaching is to have sensitive timing. And this is something that is almost impossible to teach other than through experience. The reason it is so difficult is that all timing is dependent upon, and will change with, the day, the hour, the age level of the class, the size of the class, the harmony of the class and the behavior level of the class. Also, it depends upon the individual rhythm of the person teaching the class. Experience in teaching or assisting a teacher is the only way an individual's timing can be recognized and improved. It is impossible to sense timing abstractly or theoretically.

Sensitive timing means knowing when to change from one activity to another, being aware of the length of time the average student in the class can concentrate, being able to recognize signs of boredom, fatigue, over stimulation and over expectation on the part of either the teacher or the student, and then knowing what to do about it.

The artistic or aesthetic element of teaching presents another somewhat difficult problem. This element means good taste, skill and love of beauty.

This is difficult to teach until the student is mature, sophisticated and able to appreciate the arts.

So again, with children and untrained dancers, the teacher must help them develop and grow by allowing them to experience a wide range of directed, organized movement in order to acquire greater skills.

I must emphasize that this does *not* mean that one should teach classical ballet or other such set movement styles, but rather teach, direct and organize movements that are based upon exaggerations, expansions and abstractions of the more natural ways of moving.

Perception, interpretation, and motivation are so intimate, personal and usually so flexible and unconscious, that it is unnecessary for either teacher or student to try to consciously verbalize about what is happening.

If a student moves in a variety of ways, he will have a variety of experiences. He will feel and benefit from them, but he will not necessarily be able to discuss them clearly. In fact, if he is forced to verbalize, the incorrect interpretation will often be expressed. To talk about the physical happenings and the related feelings does not in any way add to the fulfillment of the experience nor to the perfection of the movement. Only in choreography, when one is trying to interpret someone else's movement and feelings, does verbal analysis of the experience of movement have any significance or value. Then it is quite necessary.

So, with children, non-dancers and patients of all ages, the objective in Body Ego Technique is to teach goal-directed movements by organizing and structuring and broadening the range of the external movement patterns in order to help balance the physical and emotional behavior of the student. If this can happen, then the other techniques of education and profession are much more easily achieved.

Besides demonstrating and teaching definite movement patterns, there are various ways to stimulate and encourage creative movements and ideas: music, shapes, sounds. This will be explained in the class examples.

Another very important aspect of teaching is the use of the voice. Despite the importance of nonverbal communication, the teacher's voice is probably the most stimulating and the most controlling factor of any class. Because the voice is another external expression of the total self, it is an obvious example of how you feel about yourself, as well as how you feel about what you are teaching. The voice should have authority, yet also respect for others. It should not communicate anger nor be condescending. The voice should be used deliberately as much as possible in relationship to the motivation of the movements being taught. For instance, when trying to stimulate excitement, the voice should be motivated by and express excitement. When slow and smooth movements are desired, the voice should become soft and slow. When the tempo of the movement speeds up, the tempo of the voice should do the same. So, the overall quality, the tempo, the loudness or softness, the positive authority, and the sensitive changes in the voice should be deliberately governed by, or motivated by whatever your intent is in each part of the technique that you are teaching.

If the instructor of Body Ego Technique has a thorough knowledge of the materials being taught, a clear understanding as to why that material is being taught, has a clear motivation for teaching, knows the differences between reality and fantasy, enjoys teaching and can appreciate the exciting rewards of seeing the accomplishments of others, then the manner in which she teaches, the proper use of the voice and the sensitive timing, will to a large extent follow naturally.

CHAPTER 5

BODY EGO TECHNIQUE CLASSES:
INFANT—PRESCHOOL—
ELEMENTARY SCHOOL

THE SIMPLEST FORM OF Body Ego Technique is used by parents to help their infant recognize through touch and feeling different parts of his own body and eventually these same parts of another's body.

The infant needs to be touched and cuddled and picked up often. He needs to feel his body against the warmth of his mother's body. These tactile experiences cause internal sensations and postural changes.

> . . . The regularity and repetitiveness of stimulation and gratification help the infant to maintain himself outside the womb during the critical phase of his early postnatal life.

> We are struck by the way in which rhythms of various kinds become important. Rhythm is a promise of continuity. It is a promise that what is happening now will happen again and that nothing in between will shatter the chain. We posit that the infant can discriminate the rhythmic discontinuity. The startle reflex is one type of response to this discrimination. This rudimentary discrimination may also become the basis for the later attitude of trust and mistrust assumed by Erikson (1950) to be the outcome of the first stage of psychosocial development. Mistrust would be founded on an anticipation that discontinuities are bound to happen. If we assume that discontinuities in the early stages of life are inherently painful, we can come to understand that to anticipate difference or change becomes an anticipation of pain. This could explain the fear of change observable in many disturbed children who must keep their environment and routines exactly the same. An attitude of trust would be based on the confident expectation that there will be consistency in the progression of events. From the start of life consistency has become identified with pleasure and gratification. These consistencies bear the special stamp of the child's culture. Adapting oneself to the child's individual rhythms may require creative ingenuity. . . .

> Any incidental learning which takes place during this phase in which tactile experience is important will be of significance in later ego development. The capacity to cathect one's own physical boundary may be one of the incidental rewards derived from proper gratification of the tactile mode. Fragmented ego experience of severely disturbed children may be pathological manifestations of an early disturbance in the rhythm of tactile stimulation (cf. Mahler, 1952),[14]

---

[14] Howard Shevrin and Povl Toussieng, Conflict over tactile experiences in emotionally disturbed children. *J. Am Acad Child Psychiatry,* Vol. 1:4 (1962), pp. 570–571.

When the infant can identify various body parts, the teaching can continue in a more enjoyable way by adding a specific rhythm of repetitious timing to the action of touching or moving. For instance, "touch your nose-nose-nose, touch your eyes-eyes-eyes, touch your toes-toes-toes, touch your head-head-head." This would have to be repeated many times before the baby could do this touching as a continuous rhythmic action. The parent could slow the action or speed it up or vary it according to the baby's own tempo or timing as well as his physical coordination potential.

The parent can literally touch and move the hands, legs, etc. of the infant and at the same time, name the part of the body being used, such as hands "shake-shake-shake." When an infant kicks his legs, the parent can put his hands on the soles of the feet and say, "push-push-push with your legs-legs-legs." The baby will begin to feel his own body boundaries as well as the *affect* or the amount of energy or force used to accomplish this kick. He need not be consciously aware; he is feeling and learning anyway.

One can deal with space and directions by lifting the infant up high in the air and then down, up-down, high-low. The infant can be rolled from a position in which he is lying on his back, over on his side, then over on his stomach, then to his other side, over and over. Space sensations are also taking place when the infant is being rocked or bounced on the knee or leg.

Another effective way of helping the infant gain knowledge of his identity is to let him look in the mirror as soon as he can focus. He can begin to see himself as a separate being from his mother. He can begin to recognize his own individual features. He can move and see himself move.

In order to have a clear body image, one must learn not only what size and shape he is, but he must become aware of the actual body boundaries. He must learn how far he can reach, and he must learn how close he can move in locomotion towards other objects and people before touching or bumping them. When a child starts crawling, he begins to feel space and distance more clearly. The parent can help by changing positions and distances, then calling the child. Soon the child will begin to explore on his own and for his own reasons.

After the infant has gained some physical control and dexterity and his concentration span increases a bit, movements begin to take on some related perception. For instance, he learns that when he reaches he may be picked up. He learns that there are times when the adults are playful and teasing. He learns that there are times when they seem to be pleased with him and other times when they seem to be angry with him. The baby senses these feelings by the manner in which he is touched, by the amount of energy or force used and by the tempo or speed of the movements. When an infant reaches and the parent responds by picking him up, he *could* feel frightened, regardless of whether the adult was angry, or teasingly playful. The reason might be that, at this simple but sensitive perceptual level, the strength and affect behind both of these movements can feel much the same to the inexperienced infant. Another reason that these two movements can be confusing is that often there is a basic motivation of anger behind teasing or playfulness. Teasing or joking is almost always a cover-up for a deeper motivation, or it can be the externalization of an unconscious feeling.

The baby learns to wave his hand while someone else says "bye-bye," long before he really understands the related act of someone leaving. About the time he begins to understand that when you wave bye-bye, someone is leaving, he also becomes aware that the someone leaving can be his mother. Because his own body image and identity are still vague and confused with his mother's, this experience can be very frightening. Positive reinforcement is needed at this time.

The child gradually learns that when his mother does leave, there is a good chance that she will return, that when she is gone, his body is still there, that when she burns her hand, it does not burn his, and that when he touches the hot stove it will burn him. Through these kinds of repeated experiences, the child begins to recognize that he is a separate individual with a separate body. He learns that he has a special name by which he can be verbally identified. A functional knowledge of these facts is not very easily accomplished and all of us are dealing with some phase of body image recognition and self-identity throughout our lifetime. How often we hear the statement from adults, "I don't know who I am," or "I have to find myself."

Mother-child separation at the preschool level (2–5 years) if poorly handled can be traumatic. Once again, reassurance of safety in separation must be established by helping the child to recognize his separate body, his separate being, his separate identity. He must learn that he has not been abandoned and that his mother will return at the promised time. The mother must know the importance of this fear and try to work it through with the child by doing her part to ease this separation developmental step. Space, distance and organized time begin to take on meaning and importance at this stage. This separation reality can occur and recur at various times during early childhood. Some older children and even adults can have a residue of unresolved mother-child separation which can result in a lack of clarity in body image and self-identity.

When a child reaches preschool age, he can begin to handle a little more structure. A structured session of Body Ego Technique should be presented for a short period of time each day, rather than a longer time once or twice a week. This technique can also be used in a variety of ways throughout the activities of children in day care centers or in preschool and kindergarten. Again, the prime objective at this age is to facilitate the development of self-identity, body image, ego structure and ego growth.

The structured class can begin in a circle or holding on to the wall or barre for support of balance. The circle offers more security for this age level because everyone can be seen and the individual exposure and responsibility are evenly distributed. It is even easier for the child to start sitting on the floor in a circle formation. When possible, drums or other percussive instruments should be used by each child. These instruments can be an unconscious extension of the child and again this helps him to cope with his feelings, fears and with his personal exposure at this sensitive age.

This rhythmic section is valuable, not only to the child but to the teacher. The manner in which the child hits the floor or drum reveals very much about how he feels about himself and the situation. It reveals his own timing and the amount of energy or affect being felt at this particular time. The perceptive teacher can make use of the child's individual timing and the internal motivation being externalized through the use of the percussive instrument or perhaps the clapping of the hands. The rhythmic breathing is even more revealing at this age of development because it is largely involuntary and not consciously controlled. One way to help the child become more aware of his own timing is for the teacher to give a set rhythm such as 1–2/1–2/1–2, using the natural accent by saying, "Loud-soft 1–2 Loud-soft." The child's ability to imitate, hear, see and control a different timing than his own and his ability to change the timing and affect of his rhythm shows how much he is aware of and feels his own timing. When he can change and broaden his rhythmic and tempo span, he broadens his experiences. This is seldom accomplished before the fourth or fifth year of age.

To help a child recognize his name, be able to say it out loud and to feel the associated affect, the name can be clapped or beat, as the sounds in the name are being said. For instance, Mar-y, 1–2, Mar-y, Mar-y, Mar-y. John, 1–, John, John, John. Jer-e-my, 1–2–3, Jer-e-my, Jer-e-my, Jer-e-my etc.

The rhythmic breathing and handling of percussive instruments and the clapping of the hands should be carried over or continued into movement in and through space. When rhythm is emphasized as the children move through space instead of sitting, a new and different challenge is experienced. The rhythm now has to adjust to the weight and size of the child trying to move through space and his physical ability to move that weight and size at a given time.

This structured way of learning about rhythm may seem rather unrelated to body image, but is is very directly related. A child can move only within his own timing range and within his own energy range, which develop and are motivated by his own experiences (real and imagined) and the way in which he has coped with those experiences. It takes much learning, conscious and unconscious awareness of body image and self-identity, before a child is confident enough, physically and emotionally, to voluntarily experience changes that will broaden his rhythmic movement range and influence his behavior. Because a broader range of movements and thus experiences do broaden the range of behavior, and allow for a wider range of balanced stable behavior, this wider range of being makes it possible to learn more easily, whether it is reading, arithmetic, writing, or how to relate to other individuals.

Live piano accompaniment is an important addition for the remainder of the class. Music helps to keep the group together and stimulates various qualities and tempos of movement by following the teacher and the young students. If accompaniment is not available, the teacher can use a drum to accompany the class.

The warm-up of the class can be handled differently for young children. As mentioned before, young children are almost always in a state of being warmed-up. They have a fast heart beat (pulse) and are usually active enough at all times to cause the blood to circulate fast enough to keep the muscles warm and agile.

The warm-up, much like the infants', can consist of rhythmically touching and moving isolated body parts, such as, "Touch your head-head-head-head, touch your shoulders-shoulders-shoulders-shoulders, touch your knees-knees-knees-knees, touch your toes-toes-toes-toes." The whole procedure can be repeated a number of times and with different body parts being touched, perhaps letting the children suggest some of them. The rhythm and coordination can be changed or challenged by touching each separate part only once, "Touch your head-shoulders-knees-toes. 1–2–3–4." This too can be repeated and varied. This action also increases sequence memory which is important later for reading ability.

The directions, in space, of moving up and down have automatically been introduced because in order to touch the knees and toes the child must bend over. The head alone can continue this up and down direction by moving "head up-down, up-down" then "shoulders up-down, up-down," then elbows, hands, legs, feet, torso, etc. The same kind of movement can take place while the students are sitting as well as when they are standing. While standing in the circle or holding onto a barre or the wall, different *ways* or *qualities* of moving separate body parts can be introduced. The head, for instance, can *swing* from side to side covering a larger and fuller dimension of space. The arms can *swing* front and back, side to side.

Various tempos determine the amount of space that can be used as well as the amount of energy it takes to move in various ways. The faster the tempo, the smaller the movement becomes; it uses less space, but more energy or effort is needed to perform it. Children this age have a short concentration span, but they need and enjoy much repetition. Sometimes the same objectives can be approached in a variety of ways, rather than to perfect one. The class for children of this age must move along at a fast enough pace to keep within the short concentration span but allow for a feeling of accomplishment. The need of repetition, the need of the feeling of accomplishment and the short concentration span are reasons why shorter daily classes are more successful and can be kept more interesting for the children than the longer, less frequent classes.

The younger preschool child (two and three years) can remain in the circle formation for most of their class. They can learn about directions by stretching or reaching high for four counts, then drop down and hold for four counts. The teacher can deal with tempo changes and count changes, and the child will struggle to learn and usually think he has accomplished it long before he really has. Front and back can be emphasized by touching the toe out front and return, and then to the back and return without looking. This action leads into points on the floor (front, back, side) and the same off the floor.

For young children and non-dancers, it is much more sensible to use the words *small* kick, *large* or *high* kick, *small* knee bend and *deep* or *large* knee bends rather than using French ballet terms.

Sitting on the floor for stretches is safer and easier for the young child who is also struggling with balance. While sitting, leaning over the legs, if possible holding onto the ankles and pulling the head, chest and back towards the knees is one of the basic stretches. The same forward action can take place with legs open and turned out, as well as stretching over each knee. The waist has to twist in order to try to get the head down to each knee of the open legs. There are other variations on these stretches. "The abdominal lifts" are what is ordinarily called a "sit-up." Children this young have very weak abdominal muscles and usually have to have their ankles held in order to sit up. Lying back from the sitting position is equally difficult, and the child uses his elbows to break the back fall. Even children this young can use the barre or wall for support in learning some stretches and skills. To stretch the back of the thighs, called the ham strings, the child makes a flat back while holding onto the barre with both hands. The entire torso and head are on one level. He bounces against the straight legs from the hip joints. Flexibility and strength have to slowly build through repetition over a long period of time.

One of the ways to develop the strength and timing of a jump is to have the children stand facing the barre and hold on with both hands. Bounce; both knees bending, accenting the up beat such as down-UP, down-UP, and-UP, and-UP. This can be done in a series of eight. After eight bounces of the knees, add the heels lifting with the knee bounce. After eight of these, have the toes leave the floor into a jump. The landing in a jump is perhaps the most important part for the child to learn. The proper technique of the foot and knee preparation helps him to land correctly. The feet must be very flexible so that the heels touch the floor each time and the knees must bend upon landing. The rhythmic counts of eight must be fast enough so that the small, shortlegged child can attempt to fulfill them. The rhythm will eventually help him to recognize the amount of energy and the change of timing he needs to lift his own weight into the air at a given set time. Much repetition is needed to bring about this awareness and it is important not to emphasize the child's inability to sense or perfect this change of timing at this age. It is up to the teacher to do most of the adjusting by taking her cues from the children in the class.

To begin to learn how to skip is accomplished in much the same way. As soon as the child can take off on two feet (jump) he can try, with support, to hop on one foot. Teaching him to count 1–2 and do two hops on one foot is the first step. He can usually do the two hops at barre long before he can do the same two hops without support. Often he is unaware that he is, or is not, accomplishing the skip. When the child does try to skip around the room, the teacher or assistant can help by holding his hand and helping him to feel the rhythm as well as giving him physical support. One of the hops becomes the transitional step as he changes weight from one foot to the other. Repeat the action every day but do not try to perfect the skip too soon. When the child gains the strength, the coordination and the rhythm, he will skip.

Falls can also be taught to the young child. Children must be taught to protect the knees. They drop with ease, but usually do not consider or distinguish the difference between the hard wooden floor and the outdoor ground or lawn. The knee has only a thin layer of skin to protect the patella (knee cap), and that bone can be easily injured. Side falls as well as back falls are good beginning falls to teach. These falls can grow naturally and easily out of the squat, with which this young a child is still very familiar. The starting position can be the squat, and then the fall sideways onto the thigh or backwards onto the seat is simplified.

Young children, like the insecure adult, have a certain amount of fear of purposefully stretching out on the floor. This is especially true of the back fall, which puts them in a vulnerable position. They are much more at ease on their sides or bellies. The recovery from falls can also begin at this age; however, caution must be used about over-expectation. To help the child find ways to get up from the prone position takes time. The usual way of recovery is for the child to use the hands and arms for support against the floor as he pushes himself up to a sitting position and then on up to a standing position. As the leg, back and abdominal muscles strengthen, various ways of recovering from the fall can be taught.

Two- and three-year-olds are usually rather cautious about how they move, and so the discipline and limitations should be freer. On the other hand, the four- to six-year-olds are easily stimulated, often get wild and out of control, and limitations must be imposed to help them function with some balance and to protect them against hurting themselves. With boys, this limitless action seems to continue for a longer time than with girls. Directions and changes must be dealt with in movement and not with hopeful loud verbalization. For instance, if the children are running around, falling and sliding because of stimulation rather than direction, the teacher could give a sudden contrast in movement such as, "Everyone sit down and rock side to side" etc. This sort of action is much more effective than trying to point out to the children that they have gotten out of control.

Locomotor movements on the diagonal from one corner to the opposite corner can be an exposure that some children will find threatening. It is wise not to force them, but rather to give them the support of a partner or even the teacher moving with them to show them the safety of this individual experience. Always start with a simple walk. The manner of affects and posture will tell you exactly how the child feels about himself.

The walk should be formalized even for young children. It is much easier to expose yourself and to feel secure when the limitation of the form protects your behavior. To give form to the walk can be as simple as just adding a definite beginning and an ending. The beginning can be when the teacher calls the child's name and the ending could either be a hold for a given amount of time or a set curtsy or bow to designate the end of the walk across the room. This structured use of space should be repeated for all of the locomotor skills. Structure, limitations and form seem to add the security that is needed to build confidence in these young children.

By the time the child is six or seven years of age there are usually different problems. The child of this age wants to show off, wants to be first, is very easily over-stimulated and feels quite capable of teaching the class. These children are more able to clearly separate fantasy and reality and they are anxious to deal with make-believe. The younger child is not at all sure, at any time, what is fantasy and what is reality. This is one of the reasons that teasing or joking can be so cruel when used with a child under five years of age. A young child cannot tell the adult that he is frightened or that he does not understand the imposed imagery. He does not know that there is a choice.

The creative work of the preschool child will usually deal with animals, nursery rhymes, or simple fairy tales. These ideas must be taken apart for the child and dealt with as separate thoughts. For instance, if dancing about the three bears, it might be necessary to first talk about and move like bears. This is after it has been clearly established what a bear is, how heavy, how large, how slow and how safe it can be to pretend to temporarily play the part of a big, angry, scary bear and still return to being yourself.

One preschool group read about, talked about, thought about, fought about, and they each chose a favorite character and finally performed a simple version of The Wizard of Oz for their parents. The four-year-old boy who played the part of the friendly lion frightened himself to tears each time he started to roar. He always wanted to try again, and finally when he had the simple costume to wear for the performance, he was able to separate the fantasy from the reality, and he mastered that particular fear. The costume, recognizable as a separate entity for the child, was of specific value in this situation.

The creative work can be especially significant when the children *can be* a part of a group such as when taking part in dancing such a story. The younger child prefers and needs to have the support of a partner or a group when he is exposing himself in this way. The child of six years or over usually prefers to show off his individual abilities by working alone or being the main character in the story. Moving with a partner or in a group can also be an effective way to encourage the performance of the locomotor skills as well as introducing conscious social relationships. Partner and group activity also helps to expand spatial awareness and increase individual identity.

The use of colorful scarves can be a most enjoyable way to finish a class for young children. The children can dance with the scarves as the quality and tempo of the music stimulates change. They can use the scarves as an extension of themselves—such as wings—as they *pretend* to move like birds, butterflies, flies, and even airplanes. One three-year-old decided to pretend to fly like an elephant. When the teacher reminded her that elephants really do not fly, she and the entire class said, "What about Dumbo?" The teacher was again reminded of the overlapping of fantasy and reality in the mind of the very young child. The class can also finish by having the children repeat simple combinations of movements such as two children hooking right elbows, couples forming a circle, turn around each other while walking, running, galloping or, when possible, skipping. Various ways of moving with the partner can continue, or the partners can separate to do some movements and then come back together for a final curtsy or bow. The combination should be simple and short and repeated each time so that the young children can feel a sense of accomplishment.

In addition to the structured class, there are other ways in which Body Ego Technique can be used with children in preschools, nursery schools, day care centers, etc. In a child's play, you can help him to be aware of, or to recognize a beginning and an ending when running races, to sense how quickly or slowly he can move when playing games, or to feel the difference in the time it takes to walk up the steps of the slide in comparison to sliding down and to feel the variations of directions and space used to play tag, blindman's bluff, climb the jungle gym or stretch rope or to go up and down and over and under and through an obstacle course. Jumping on the trampoline is fun and includes broad elements of space, timing, courage and accomplishment.

In all of these activities the objectives of Body Ego Technique are consciously secondary because the main objective for the child is to win the race or to prevent being "It" or caught or to safely make it through the obstacle course in the given amount of time.

Shapes and letters and numbers can be drawn on the sidewalk or on the floor with chalk. The children can identify the different shapes by perhaps jumping into them as the teacher verbally identifies the letter, the number, the triangle, the square or circle, etc. The various shapes can be moved by a choice of activity such as skip the circle, run the number 6 and jump the letter A. This sort of learning should be limited and dropped by the time the child is ready for kindergarten. By this time, the shapes and letters and numbers should take on more realistic academic and symbolic meanings and not be confused with the reality of the body and its functional purposes.

Body Ego Technique for children of the elementary school age (6–12) includes all of the activities of the preschool child as well as many variations and developments of these basic movement patterns. One difference is the manner in which the material is presented by the teacher. The concentration span of a child at this age is greatly increased, and consequently an activity can develop further and be much more interesting for the child. The greatest difference that the teacher must be aware of and deal with is the amount of sophistication that each added year of age seems to produce. This can be seen not only in the growing capacity of physical muscle strength, flexibility and coordination, but also in the external expression of creative and exciting thought processes.

It seems interesting that, without fail, between the ages of 9 years and 12 years there begins to be a distortion or confusion about one's body image. The girls become quite round shouldered to hide the developing breast or the lack of it. Creative modern dance or Body Ego Technique suddenly seems unbelievably ugly and undesirable. Ballet, toe shoes, and tutus become so important in comparison to bare feet, leotards and tights. After dealing with a few years of feeling personal rejection and failure as a teacher each time this happened, I began to explore the reasons for this change.

Classical ballet is as far removed from reality as possible. It is almost totally technique or step learning oriented. The objective at all times in every class is to perfect the technique and to do it, if possible, exactly as the teacher or some former dancer has executed it. There is little or no emphasis on individuality.

In creative modern dance the technique is learned to be used as an exposure of one's individual expression. An exposure of oneself is not easy to handle when one is developing and physically maturing faster than he or she can adjust to the changes that are taking place. The need to hide behind or get lost in the classical ballet technique at this age is, in most instances, approached and dealt with on an unconscious level. It is also interesting that if a dancer continues his studies as a professional or nonprofessional, he returns to modern dance as soon as he has a clearer and more acceptable body image and identity. This usually occurs between the ages of sixteen and twenty.

These children of elementary school age can use props advantageously, and they can express both fantasy and reality through a simple form of the art of dance. They adore mastering and showing off their technical feats and they have unbelievable freedom and courage in handling this form of expressive communication. Perhaps it should be mentioned again that the form, the structure and the limitations that provide boundary lines help to broaden the range of the freedom of expression.

These positive remarks and the teaching approach mentioned apply to the average so-called normal child. The percentage of children who have problems and need special attention and help unfortunately seems to be extremely high.

The children with emotional and physical problems also need to establish a body image and a self-identity. The approach is much the same and the adjustments and changes can be most effectively handled by the instructor. The teacher's sensitive timing, empathy and encouragement can make the difference between failure and success when teaching students of any age with or without physical or emotional problems.

CHAPTER 6

BODY EGO TECHNIQUE CLASSES: NON-DANCERS—PROFESSIONAL DANCERS

CLASSES FOR NON-DANCER adolescents and adults become increasingly more interesting and challenging. Some adolescents can still be struggling to establish a different body image than the one that they had in early childhood. Unless the student of this age has been quite active throughout earlier years, his physical movement range, especially that of flexibility, will have decreased. Muscles can lose strength and flexibility rather quickly or they may not develop beyond the limited requirements of the average functional purposes. This could also mean that the individual's experiences have been equally limited.

The basic class material has its roots in the early childhood class material. The variations and developments are dependent upon the capabilities of the students in the class. Unlike the class for young children, warm-up is extremely important for these older students, to prevent injury while they stretch and build muscle strength. They can also enjoy the drill techniques that lead towards physical and emotional confidence because they do have a longer concentration span and more physical endurance than either younger or older students. The emotional content of the movements and the thought processes are more sophisticated and offer a broader range of motivation. In these classes, as in all other classes, the basic and first objectives are to establish a sense of individual rhythm, body image and self-identity.

The majority of adolescents and adults differ in another way from the younger student. They prefer to deal with learned techniques only, because, as mentioned before, after early childhood we feel less and less able to use imagination and fantasy in a constructive way. Even though the motivation *always* incites or prompts the action, it does not always have to be consciously dealt with in a technique class. It takes much courage and confidence and a sense of well-being to voluntarily expose one's inner thoughts and feelings by externalizing them into dance and movement.

Because there should be evidence of some maturity by this age, it is more obvious when there is residue of an unresolved childhood developmental step, fixed postures or ways of moving or when one is functioning at

43

a regressed level. The average normal adolescent or adult does have some such problems, but they usually are not exaggerated enough to interfere with his everyday functioning. Sometimes these problems are called phobias or personality traits.

Classes for non-dancers, teenagers and adults should be divided into beginning, intermediate and advanced levels, as they are for younger children. If the older student has not had previous dance or movement experience, he will have to start at the beginning. There are advanced students and there are advanced professional performing dancers. It is possible to be an advanced dancer or teacher in the academic field without also being an advanced performing professional dancer. The universities have recognized this and have tried to bridge the gap by bringing in performing artists to teach classes and to choreograph for the university students. However, that is not the answer. There is only one way to learn the art of performing on a professional level, and that is to experience professional performance. Academic student performances are not professional nor do they produce professional artists. The subtle difference is difficult to explain in words. A professional is so dedicated to his art that it would be impossible for him to deal with, in either time or divided interest, the necessary fulfillment of the academic involvement of the student. The student cannot allow himself to be as dedicated as is necessary to bring about a professional attitude.

When a performing professional teaches in the academic world he loses a certain element of his creativity. The reality situation detracts from the fantasy of the theatrical world of make-believe. If possible, performing and teaching should be done at different times in one's career. Performing experience does broaden the range of teaching ability. It broadens the possibility of making good use of the imagination, fantasy, and most of all, objectivity.

The professional artists prefer not to deal with too much reality. Perhaps this is one of the reasons they have agents or managers to handle the reality situations and to make decisions. Some professional performers have a difficult time handling reality at all, and they escape by functioning most of the time within the unreal world of their art. Role playing can become such a way of life for the artist that self-identity can become confused. Much insecurity and fear is disguised by artistic temperamental tantrums.

To some, it might seem that, in these aspects of handling reality, there is a narrow line between the professional artist and the psychotic. However, the well-functioning artist is able to recognize the great value in being able to use the world of fantasy voluntarily in the service of the ego and can feel safe in returning to and functioning in the real world. The artist uses the form to deal with reality. He can make statements about his likes or dislikes, he can be angry or sad or happy and through his art express these ways of being. Because he is an artist and effectively uses the form in the right environment, he is protected by society. Much like the young child at play, the performer acts out his feelings over and over, which allows him to master those feelings and to gain control of the situation.

One might even speculate whether all artists would be psychotic if they did not have the ability to use their art to express their desires and frustrations.

The psychotic continually confuses fantasy and reality and often acts out an unacceptable fantasy wish or fear within the reality environment. He is not protected in the same way as the artist and he usually has to be separated from society. In other words, the artist purposefully vacillates between fantasy and reality while the psychotic totters back and forth involuntarily. This is an important difference.

Classes for the professional can be much more verbal. The vocabulary and many of the techniques have been codified by this time. The material is only as limited as the teacher presenting the class. The professional is experienced enough to perform class techniques in combinations of movements. Most professionals do a good warm-up before class begins. They know their bodies well and they each know how much preparation is needed. Usually the emphasis in a professional class is on technique. The emotional content, when possible, is purposefully separated from the physical movement techniques and is reserved for individual personal communication in choreographies. In Body Ego Technique, creative modern dance or contemporary dance, group choreographics also demand individual interpretations. Ballet is different because the *same* techniques are used to interpret many different ideas or musical scores. In each classical ballet, there is also a corps de ballet, which is a chorus or group performing the same movements at the same time. This does occur, but less often in modern dance choreography. Because of the proficiency of the advanced professional, much material can be covered in each class. Such classes are usually directed rather than being taught. Daily work is necessary to keep the artist in top condition, and most professional classes are taken for this purpose. The professional dancer uses the highest form of organization. The total being is the tool used for this art.

> . . . There are the more intricate movements used by the highly trained professional dancer. Here we begin to see even more complex aspects of communication. The professional dancer draws upon the same basic movements and emotions, but abstracts and formalizes them. Now we have proceeded to levels of communication which approximate the symbolic processes of language used to express abstract thought. It represents one form of ultimate mastery of those primitive processes which are more simply instinctual or irrational, transformed into deliberate, formal, symbolic modes of communication. Dance remains physical in its mode of expression, but it is essentially conceptual in its nature. It is a higher level of organization. It synthesizes all previous forms of expression in a more meaningful way, and is capable of expressing more complex concepts.

> Movement is a universal language. We all use it. We all understand it.[15]

---

[15] *Film 'Body Ego Technique'* by Salkin-Salkin-Schoop.

CHAPTER 7

BODY EGO TECHNIQUE CLASSES: DEAF—BLIND—MENTALLY RETARDED—CULTURALLY DEPRIVED

C LASSES FOR THE EMOTIONALLY DISTURBED, the mentally ill, the educationally handicapped, the autistic child, the retarded, the culturally deprived, the deaf, the blind and the elderly, all call upon the same basic materials used in the preschool classes to accomplish the same basic objectives. The variations in the classes of Body Ego Technique seem to somewhat parallel the cycle of the normal aging process. This cycle goes from infancy to childhood to adolescence to adulthood and maturity and then back to adolescence to childhood and infancy before death. The conditions of these different age levels can occur at various times during the cycle. For instance, childish or senile behavior does not necessarily occur only when an individual is chronologically young or very old. When teaching Body Ego Technique, the manner in which the class is presented, the expectations, the involvement, the age level, the potential of the students and the desired end results make up the subtle differences.

Individuals with psychological problems have to be approached in a similar way to the infant, young child or beginning student. They may or may not have gone through a more mature stage of their life's cycle but they must now be approached at the level where they are functioning.

The *deaf* child is usually more active and physically aggressive than the average child who can hear, or the blind child. He is easily overstimulated. When teaching the deaf it is necessary to be warm but firm and to be able to direct the activity into constructive learning experiences. The preschool deaf children at the John Tracy Clinic in Los Angeles learned nonverbally and performed the Christmas story about Mary, Joseph and Jesus for their parents. Older children at the Marlton School for the Deaf in Los Angeles, also learned and performed a complete musical play.

The blind, especially children, are cautious about moving with any degree of abandon. They seem to be afraid to use space or to move at a fast tempo. Much of both physical and verbal encouragement is needed to teach them to trust you and to help them find some security within themselves and their environment. Often it is necessary to literally touch and move the blind students in order to initiate movement involvement or to help them to *feel* the external motivation. One of my assistant teachers, during a workshop being taught at Fairview State Hospital, in Costa Mesa, California, tried to teach a blind, retarded, overweight adolescent boy how to jump. She jumped with him, she held his hand and lifted his arm on each jump. She kept telling him to jump. He did not jump, he did not know how to begin to jump; he did not know what a jump looked like or how it felt to jump. Proceeding on the basis of a great deal more experience, I intuitively placed a hand on each of the boy's hips and did a repetitious rhythmic up and down motion as I rhythmically repeated the word jump. The first time I almost lifted him, and the second or third time he jumped, apparently for the first time in his sixteen years of life. He was so pleased that he continued to jump for some time. We all learned a great deal from this experience.

The use of bamboo reeds for rhythm proved to be very effective with these blind students. I taped together about six cut reeds to make this percussion instrument. I needed an instrument that would be less expensive and less dangerous with less possibility of disintegration. (Figs. 89, 90, 91) These beaters, as I called them, could be held in the hands of each individual. The students could feel the vibration as they hit the beaters against the floor. They could feel their own rhythm and hear the rhythm of the others. They could repeat their names as they felt and heard the number of sounds of each individual name. It was exciting for them as well as for us to have them listen and be able to come in on the proper beat when it was their turn. I originated these bamboo beaters many years ago when I could not afford drums for all of the children in the normal dancing classes. The lightness in weight made it possible to carry large numbers of them when I was travelling to distant schools and hospitals. The young deaf children and the mentally ill children often throw the beaters or tear them apart. The lightness makes them less dangerous, and with a little work, the broken ones can be replaced. I might add here that many so-called normal children hit the drums with such force that they too destroy good instruments very quickly, and it is best to use bamboo beaters for all classes.

Incidentally, the multiply-handicapped student with many physical limitations and the neurotic or disturbed adolescent with exaggerated emotional and motivational limitations are the biggest problems when teaching Body Ego Technique. The overall objectives remain the same, but the objective of establishing rapport and stimulating the student into full participation takes precedence over all other objectives. In most other classes these basic objectives can be accomplished along with the routine activities as the class proceeds.

In the many years I have been teaching modern creative dance I have taught deaf children, blind children, psychotic, schizophrenic, retarded and emotionally disturbed children, as well as normal children. Most of these normal children came from average to moderately high income families. The Head Start Program made it possible for me for the first time to work with an entire group of underpriviliged children. I had a feeling that because of a lack of social orientation, these children might be more fearful of adults who were unfamiliar to them and also might be reluctant to undertake new experiences. However, the exceptions were not any more numerous than among any other groups of children. And I was genuinely surprised at the freedom of expression these children had.

When I gave them directions and they understood what was wanted, they nearly all responded in a much more original and creative way than most so-called average children do. They did not seem as limited by preconceived ideas of how they should express a feeling or thought. They did not seem to feel the pressure of some nebulous idea of how they were supposed to act. They wanted to please me, and when they found out how well pleased I was with whatever they did, they became more and more confident and expressive.

When I asked them to express a feeling, they suggested the idea of being afraid and also of scaring each other, which delighted them. They all wanted to be monsters or to be chased by a monster. The few children who at first did not want to cooperate saw how much fun the others were having within the discipline of the class and usually ended up joining the group and taking their turns.

Most of the children were not consciously aware of the isolated parts of the body. Very few seemed able to find the elbows or the shoulders. The fact that there were movable joints at the wrist, elbows, and ankles was apparently new to all of them. Most could jump on both feet but an unusually large number of them lacked the physical strength and control to hop on one foot. The ones that could hop found it an easy development into a skip. To turn did not seem to be as natural and easy a movement for these children as I had assumed it was for all children. I wondered if perhaps a lack of space at home in which to turn would have anything to do with the apparent lag in this area of development.

When I gave the class a choice of ways to move across the room, most of them chose to run. They ran with great enthusiasm. Their other favorite choices among kinds of movement were rolling on the floor and jumping. One little girl said she would do a slide—I suppose because I had mentioned it as a possible choice. However, when her turn came, she started to move, hesitated, then looked at me and said, "But I don't know how to slide." I showed her how to slide and then did it with her, which made her very happy. This developed into partner work, and they all learned to slide facing a partner.

The children seemed to be at ease when the spatial directions were to go forward or up and down, but moving sideways or backwards seemed unfamiliar to them.

The group relationship was especially good. In some of the groups, a number of children did not speak English. It seemed to make very little difference so long as I demonstrated the movements and they could imitate. When I asked for creative ideas or attempted to stimulate the action verbally, we ran into a problem in communication. However, in most instances one of the children who could speak both English and, say, Spanish (the language most used here in Los Angeles) would explain to his companions what I wanted before I could even ask for help. In a few instances where there was no translator handy I would utilize gesture and pantomime to convey what I wanted, and invariably there was a satisfactory response.

Another problem in communication was brought about by terminology. Not only the terminology of dance was strange to these children but also the specialized use of words such as 'soft' in relation to rhythm. When I asked them to start the class with a very soft beat, one little boy seated next to me, lifted his foot and said, "I have soft feet. Feel!" Within seconds the entire group gathered around for me to feel their soft feet.

A 'beat' had a different meaning for most of the children. The bamboo reeds used for rhythm are called 'beaters.' When I asked the children to hit the floor with the beaters, some were frightened and asked, "Are they for beatings?" After that was clarified the children were delighted to be allowed to hit the floor as hard and as loud as they wanted. This brought smiles to all, and many asked to repeat this over and over.

Because I taught at a different center each day I had an unusual opportunity to observe the different teacher-child relationships. The teachers were as varied as any group of individuals. What I found surprising was how clearly one could see the influence the various teachers had upon these young children. Within a few weeks the overall attitude and emotional climate of each group was a reflection of the teacher in charge. For example, when the teacher was nervous or impatient or over-anxious, the children seemed to respond in like manner. When the teacher appeared calm and relaxed and under control, the children seemed to feel more at ease and better able to take instructions. Even the cleanliness and general appearance of the physical environment appeared to be reflected in the children.

I found that some of the teachers had a tendency to label the children, to place them into conventionally defined categories. I was sometimes told when I arrived at a center that "this is a shy child, this one is wild, this one is afraid, this one is disturbed, and this one won't talk." This was often said or implied in front of the child, and the child seemed obligated to live up to his label.

In one instance when an over-anxious teacher realized that I was working with, and giving special attention to, what she considered a 'disturbed child,' she quickly removed the child from the group, saying, "This is the disturbed one." It was my feeling in this instance that he was not interfering with the group and that he could have benefited very much by remaining in the group. In another instance, the teacher was under so much self-imposed control that when she saw I had stimulated the group into freely expressing fear and they became very involved in first scaring each other and then reacting with pretended fright, she almost panicked and asked, "Are you almost finished?" It is possible that she was unaware of my ability to control the situation, or perhaps she was too fearful of this kind of freedom.

There were only a few places where the facility or building made for a good class. The sites were usually in the basements of churches, with little or no air, and with a cement floor which lacked resilience.

On the whole, my feeling is that this first summer of the Head Start Program was enormously successful.

The techniques used for these children are the same basic elements found in all movement and dance. These elements are designed to educate or reeducate the individual:

1. To discover his body boundaries.
2. To help establish a body image.
3. To a recognition of self as related to others.
4. To focus the eyes, the body, the thought or idea, as well as the whole intention.
5. To experience change, change of physical posture and movement and consequently change of emotional experience.
6. To see, hear, feel and control one's own rhythm and to establish a clear boundary between make-believe and reality.

The class is structured with disciplined freedom. Part of the class is movement technique that helps to develop both a physical and emotional balance. Also I try to stimulate creative thoughts, both make-believe and real, and help the child find the movements or forms needed to express his thoughts. I try to help him to become aware of how he is moving and thinking by utilizing these thoughts and actions, be it shyness, embarrassment, silliness or fear. The feeling of being accepted as you are seems to be important to the growth of a child.

In general, children between the ages of four and five are very much the same. They are curious, anxious to learn, anxious to please, anxious to be loved and accepted. Some are cautious and afraid, some are over-active and challenging. They all seem to be searching for ways to handle themselves in a world that threatens to overwhelm them. And, consciously or unconsciously they all seem to have the same objectives—the need to be loved, to be accepted.

Children need help in developing their growing bodies. They have to develop muscle strength and tone, coordination and control. They need to find ways to allow their normal curiosity and creativeness to develop and grow. They must explore the world of make-believe in order to clearly distinguish between make-believe and reality. A child must learn that he has a separate body from others, a name that is his. He must learn that his body has separate parts and that these parts have names and can be moved separately. He must learn that he alone can control these parts as well as controlling himself as a whole. He must develop an idea of how he looks, an awareness of his body image. He must know his relationship to space, to objects and to others. He has to learn that he has his own individual rhythm or timing and his own way or quality of moving. He must learn that his rhythm and quality are determined by the emotional affect with which he responds or reacts. He must learn self-discipline and control. He must have respect for himself and for others. He must learn to obey and still be free and confident enough to initiate ideas and thoughts and contribute to the society in which he lives.

It is a difficult job and every child needs as early a head start as he can get.

The emotionally disturbed, the educationally handicapped, the mentally ill, the culturally deprived and sometimes the autistic child are almost always potentially much more capable than their current ways of functioning might indicate. In these groups, when retardation is not a factor, you can find a rather good muscle tone, and usually a somewhat alert posture and movement patterns that seem to almost contradict their behavior. It is not necessary to talk down to them. They can learn rather quickly, and they will progress more rapidly than one might expect. The teacher should use and demonstrate more physical nonverbal stimulation instead of depending upon possibly meaningless verbalization. Verbal connotation is varied in every situation but can be more so in these classes.

Mentally retarded individuals and the elderly should be approached in a much slower and less active way. More repetition than usual is necessary in order for them to learn. The elderly are not too anxious to move, so gentle but firm encouragement must be used in these classes. A slow, easy but very thorough warm-up should be given. Meaningful affect seems to be lacking for these individuals as they try to externalize their feelings. An important overall objective in these sessions is to deal with the appropriateness of affect as it relates to their behavior.

Sometimes the retarded, but more often the neurotic or elderly, show marked degrees of functional disorder and they may be depressed or hysterical. These exaggerated conditions call for an added dimension of calm patience on the part of the instructor. These are the times when an assistant is really a necessity. It is foolish and ineffective to try to teach alone when the class has students of varied levels and conditions who require individual attention and encouragement.

The teacher should try not only to utilize the movements and special conditions within the class but also to enter into the various individuals' movement patterns, even bizarre ones, and try to lead them into a change of movement and thus a change of experience. Individual sessions may allow this approach to be more easily accomplished. The objectives are to *rebuild ego strength, body image* and *self-identity*. Secondly, to stimulate a sense of fun and accomplishment. These important objectives can be, and usually are, fulfilled without conscious awareness or verbal discussion on the part of the patients.

Exaggerated body postures, positions and movements can be seen most clearly in classes of the more disturbed individuals. The older a person is or the longer he has had a fixed posture and way of moving, the more he becomes simple, obvious, immovable, abstract and more like a caricature.

Such clear distortions offer the instructor of Body Ego Technique a specific entrance into the person's "set" condition. For example, if a person is rocking in agitation, with hands twitching in anxiety, with an angry forward head and a tense facial expression, it is not necessary to try to analyze whether or not he is angry at someone in particular and whether he may be afraid if he stops rocking that he might attack someone. It is not necessary to know when all of this manifestation began to set in. It *is* important that the instructor recognizes in general the content of these kinds of movements and therefore use whatever approach is necessary to gain rapport in order to guide him into logical changes of movement or to develop the movement patterns he is repeating over and over. After this set posture and movement pattern has been changed and broadened, then the approach is much the same as in the other classes. In other words, use a broad diagnosis of these exaggerated positions for the purpose of making the preliminary steps and to recognize the quality and the timing from which you can expand your work with the person.

Developmentally speaking, each person is the product of his real and imagined experiences and of the way in which he has coped with these experiences, with some residue of such experience remaining as a part of his conscious or unconscious being. For this approach, it is not necessary to try to learn about all of those experiences and how and why the final manifestations took form. But it is important to use these observations to influence the manner in which you utilize the elements of movement to guide these fixed bodies into different ways of being.

This is the objective of Body Ego Technique, first, last, and always, whether teaching new experiences to the developing infant or young child, or whether you are teaching the academic student how to learn and maintain important growing experiences. If you are directing the advanced professional performer to continue to function with a clear self-concept, or if you are teaching less than normal individuals to recall old and establish new growth producing experiences, the objective remains the same.

Even though the objectives, techniques, methods and end results are similar, there are subtle differences in each class that depend upon where the students are to begin with, and the results desired by both students and instructor. Since these differences are subtle, they are not easily handled and it is a rare teacher who can teach each of the different groups equally well. Some teachers may have better rapport with young children, others with older students, others with professionals and still others may be most comfortable using this technique as a form of treatment for psychiatric patients. This technique can be used as effectively in each and all of these areas.

One of the most interesting, exciting and rewarding projects exploring the use of Body Ego Technique as therapy was carried out with chronic schizophrenic patients at Camarillo State Hospital. This project was sponsored by the State of California Department of Mental Hygiene.

The first work at the hospital was on a once-a-week volunteer basis for a period of four years. We were two women therapist-dancers and we worked with children in the mornings and with adults in the afternoon. We alternated with one teaching the class while the other one tried to encourage the patients and keep the group together. Some of the children literally climbed the walls of the large gymnasium where we first held the classes. Some of the adults would lie down in the middle of the room and refuse to move. In our ignorant enthusiasm, for these first four years we tried to cope with groups of 30 to 60 patients at a time, similar only in that they were all psychotic. In spite of the seemingly unorganized situation there appeared to be some noticeable changes among these patients.

The research director of the hospital became interested in what we were doing and supported exploration of the use of the technique on a more concentrated basis.

Having learned the hard way, we cut the size of the groups to eight patients. At first the classes were taught three days a week, all day on Monday, Wednesday and Friday. We soon recognized that the patients had a difficult time sustaining their interest and retaining the effect of the classes when there was an interruption every other day. Accordingly, the next two and a half years the classes were taught every morning except Saturday and Sunday. There was always a feeling of some regression on Monday but this five-day-a-week schedule proved to be much more effective.

The 120 patients chosen for the research project were men and women between the ages of 20 and 40, chronic schizophrenics who had been hospitalized for at least five years and some of them had been in the hospital for as long as 25 years.

Some of the sessions were for individual treatment (about 15 or 20 minutes). Other treatment was in groups usually for 45 minutes to an hour. Although these groups were small, we always had and needed the two therapists. There was still a need for individual attention and encouragement the teacher could not provide while trying to keep the group functioning as a group. After one year of teaching one group of men and one of women separately, we combined these two particular groups. The women dominated the men, who were doing very well when working separately, and the men began to regress rather quickly. It seemed that the men in general responded to the two women therapists far better than the women did. We had hoped, but it was not possible, to have a male therapist to see if the women would be more responsive than they had been to us.

The individual sessions allowed for a much closer and more meaningful contact with the therapist.

Within the various groups of patients there were exaggerated behavior patterns, exaggerated fixed postures and some very bizarre movements. One patient had a rhythmic, repetitious, seemingly choreographed, set movement pattern that he did over and over each day. The movement pattern included a sort of salute with his fingers making like devil ears, a wipe of his brow and then a bow. He usually accompanied these movements with a verbal "Merry Christmas." He was a charming person and he allowed us to enter into and repeat this movement pattern with him. He was able to become aware of what he was doing and did discuss various reasons why he did them and what they meant to him. It allowed us to make good contact with him and he did improve enough to leave the hospital and go into a limited work situation.

As explained before, these exaggerated visible, externalized movements indicate the level of development or regression the patient might have reached at this time. They provide the therapist with a definite way to contact the patient on the level where he is functioning and therefore be more effective in directing him into changes of experience. This direct approach might also be a contributing factor to my opinion that it is easier to contact and work with the more psychotic patient than it is to work with the more nearly normal or neurotic individual. It seems that the patient who is further removed from reality is, in a way, more simple, child-like or trusting and does not make the sort of judgments or evaluations of their acts as do the less disturbed patients. The sicker patients are more cooperative in general, learn through imitation much as the young child does, and they do not seem to need to evaluate the meaning of the movements.

The classes in the research project were very much like the classes given to the normal preschool child. The short concentration span is similar in both groups. The interest and naivete is similar in both groups. The thought processes in the young child have or are developing to about the same level most of the schizophrenic patients have regressed to, and the movement skills have developed or regressed to about the same level in both groups. Of course, this stage of development or education is normal for the young child. Although the learning process is similar, through the use of repetitious movement and imitation, the young healthy child learns each task more quickly and the developmental step is more meaningful to the growing ego structure than for the patient who has to recall the movements and their related experiences before he can utilize them in the service of the ego.

PART II

PHOTOGRAPHS

Ernest E. Reshovsky and Leo Salkin

To understand movement, as I have indicated previously, you must experience it; you must do it. Other than by direct physical involvement, the closest we can come to approximating the feel and pulse and flow of movement is through motion pictures. Next best is the still photograph which selects out of a continuum of movement a single image and freezes it in time and space. It provides a counterpoint to the verbal descriptions.

The photographs in the following section illustrate a number of types of movement that are rooted in infancy and continue as part of the basic movement pattern of all human beings.

I have found, during my many years of teaching varied groups of people, that these early childhood basic movements are functioning to one degree or another at every age or developmental level in which there exists some element of life.

Most of the photographs show several developments of one movement, starting from the basic or elemental form and then illustrating its growing complexity consummated in a highly sophisticated form as utilized in dance.

The photographs of the patients show them learning or relearning the elemental movements at their basic developmental stage.

By the juxtaposition of photographs of the same movement as experienced by people of different ages and for different reasons, we can see more clearly the universality of these basic movements.

Dancers: Lia Rudnick and Jeanette Salkin

Baby Experiencing Space

Retarded Girl Experiencing Space

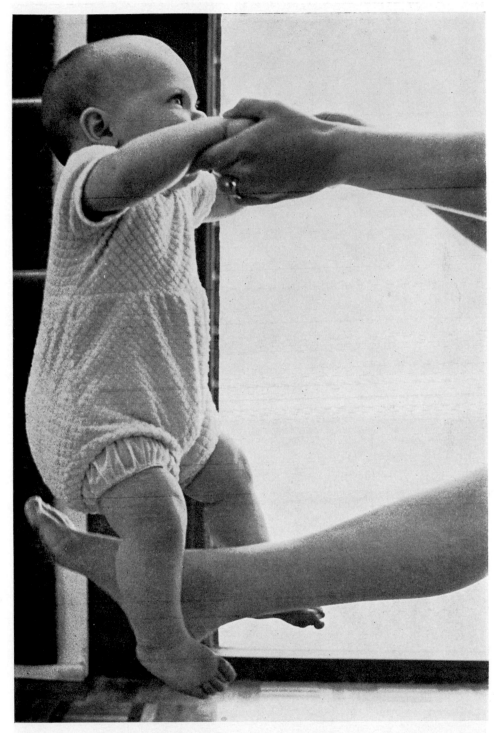

Baby Experiencing Space

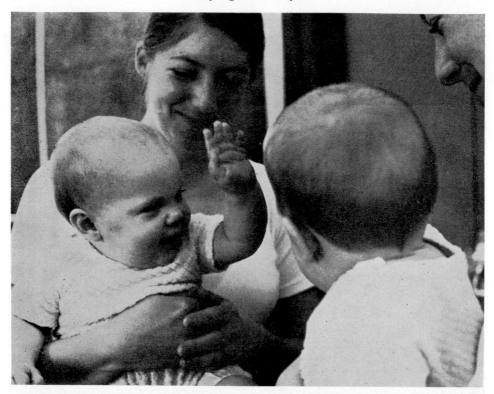

Baby Seeing Her Image

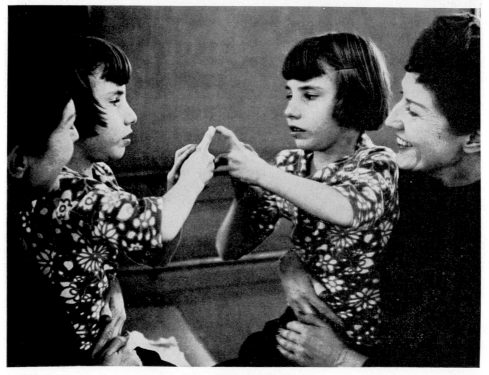

Autistic Girl Seeing Her Image

Psychiatric Patient Seeing His Image

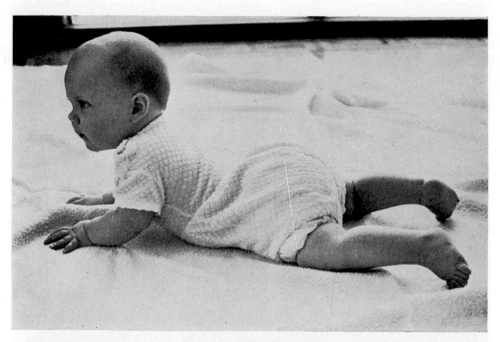

Baby Experiencing the Floor

Young Boy Experiencing the Floor

Young Girl Experiencing the Floor

Autistic Girl Experiencing the Floor

Dancer Experiencing the Floor

Psychiatric Patient Experiencing the Floor

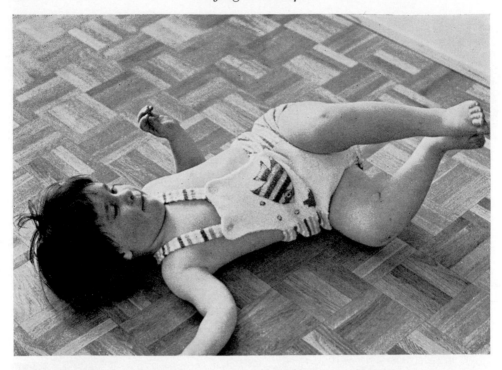

Young Girl Rolling

Psychiatric Patient Rolling

Dancer Rolling

Baby Creeping

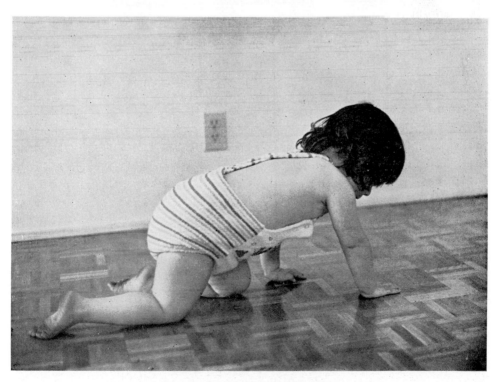

Young Child Creeping

Dancer Creeping

Dancer Creeping

Young Boy Squatting and Starting to Stand

Young Boy Walking

Boy Walking

Dancer Walking

Young Boy Running

Young Girl Running

Boy Running

Teacher & Psychiatric Patient Running

Dancer Running

Boy Galloping

Retarded Girl Galloping

Dancer Galloping

Psychiatric Patient and Teacher Galloping

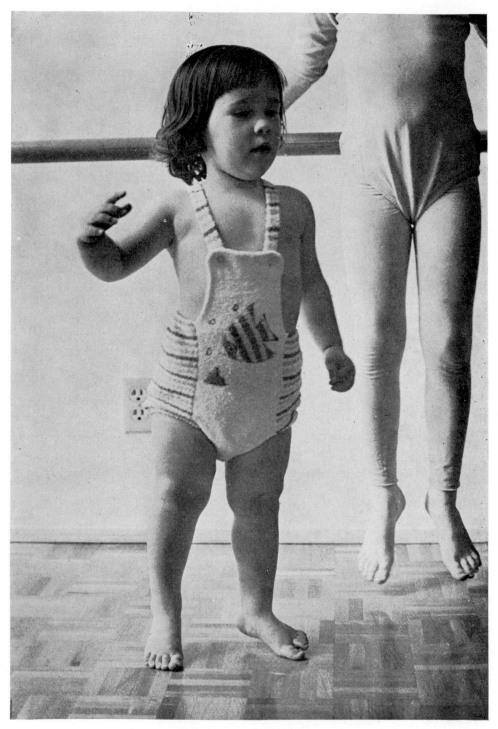

Children Jumping

Dancer Jumping

Boy Jumping

Dancer Jumping

Boy Jumping

Dancer Jumping

Young Girl Turning   *Young Boy Turning*

Psychiatric Patient and Teacher Turning

Retarded Girl Turning   Dancer Turning

Boy Hopping

Dancer Hopping

Young Child Falling

Boy Falling

Dancer Falling

Boy Skipping

Dancer Skipping

Boy Leaping

Dancer Leaping

Teacher and Child Sliding

Dancer Sliding

Psychiatric Patient and Teacher Pushing

Psychiatric Patient and Teacher Rocking

Boy Gesturing 'Hi'

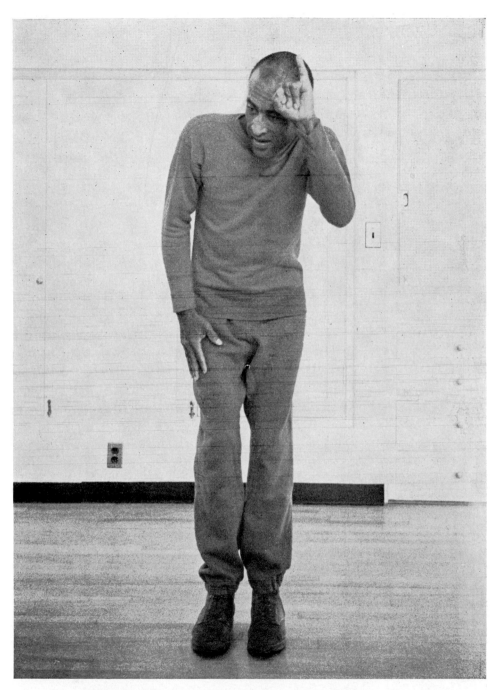

Psychiatric Patient Gesturing 'Good Morning, Sir'

Group Stretching, Jumping and Using Percussive Instruments

Children Moving in Space, Using Percussive Instruments

Psychiatric Patients and Teacher Reaching Toward a Center

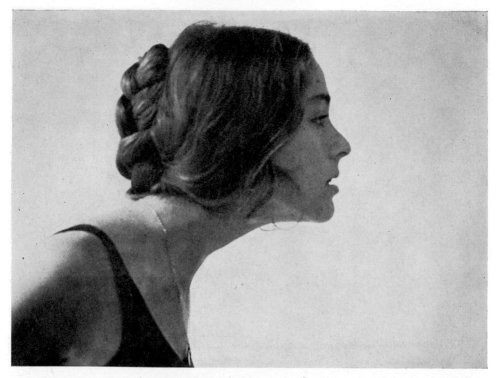

Dancer Demonstrating Exaggerated Body Postures:
Forward Aggressive Head—Head Withdrawn in
Shyness or Fear

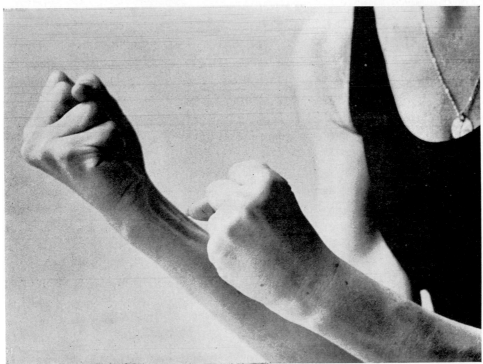

Nervous Twitching Hands—Angry Fists

*Exaggerated Body Postures—Arrogant Walk
and Ambivalence
(Split Position with Forward Aggressive Head
but Withdrawn Arms and Torso)*

Exaggerated Body Postures
Contracted Withdrawn Drooping

Psychiatric Patient Trying to Show Happiness

*Teacher Trying to Stimulate Happiness
Among Psychiatric Patients*

Young Child Showing Anger

Girl Showing Anger

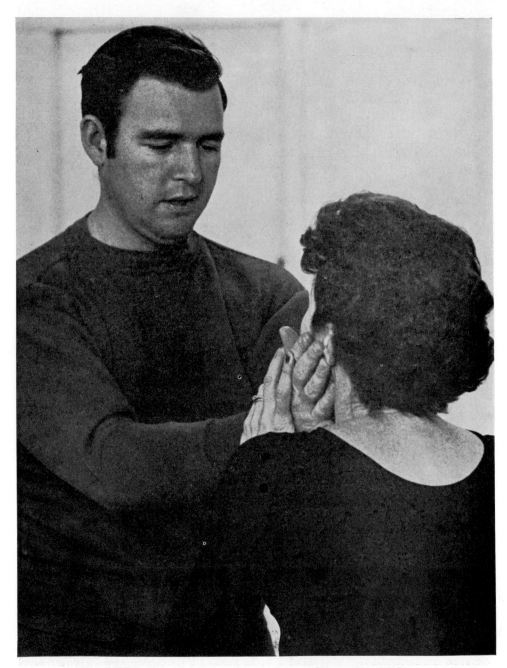

Psychiatric Patient Touching Teacher Shows

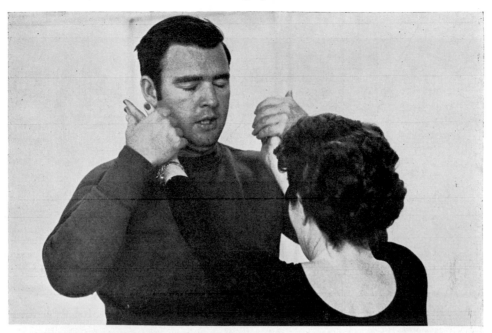

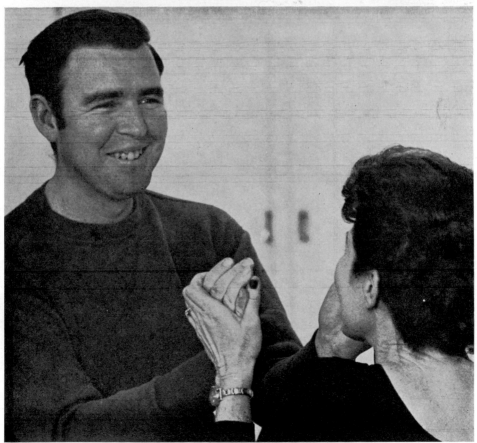

Apprehension . . . Fear . . . and Relief

Autistic Child Showing Affection

Mother and Child Showing Tenderness

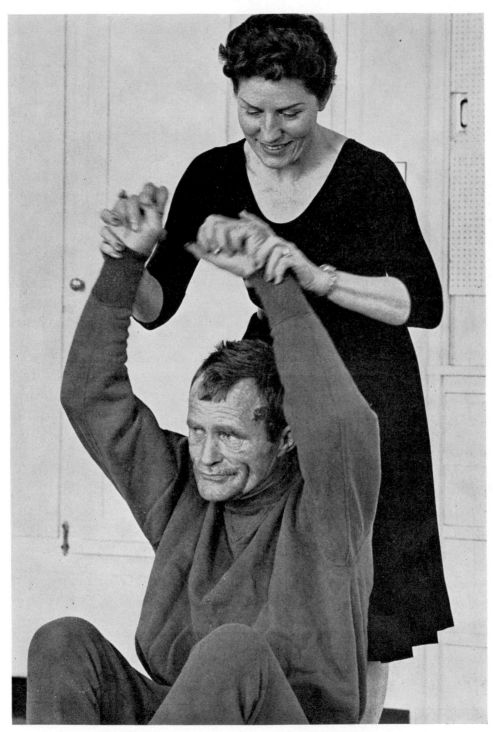

Psychiatric Patient Showing Reluctance

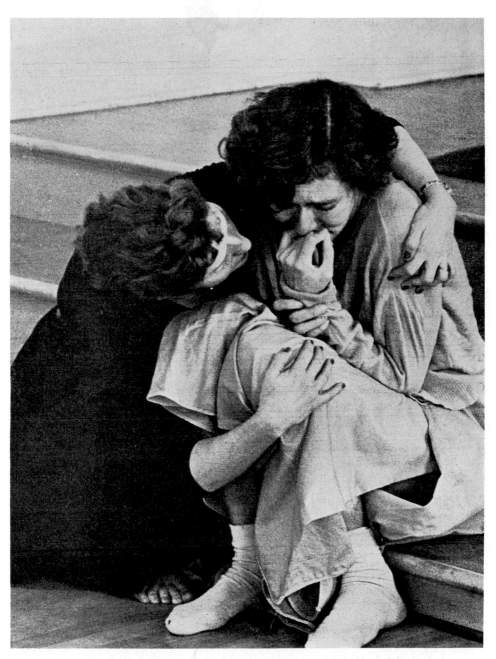

Teacher Comforting Sad Psychiatric Patient

*Baby's Body Position and Facial Expression Seem
to Indicate a Questioning, 'What's Going On?'*

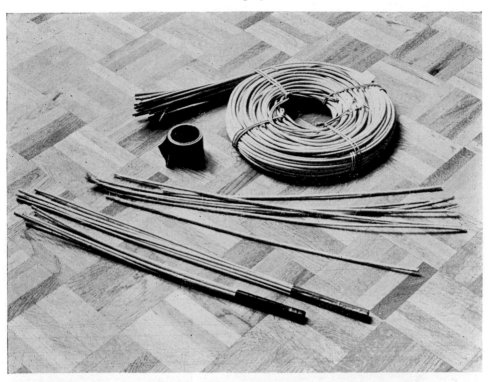

Bamboo Rhythm Beaters. The Original Form in Roll . . .

Taping the Cut Reeds . . .

Using the Beaters for Rhythm

CHAPTER 8

TEACHER TRAINING CLASS
BODY EGO TECHNIQUE

IN CONSIDERING the various qualities that have contributed to my ability as a teacher, the most valuable seems to be an awareness of myself—a knowledge and acceptance of myself—a sense of my own body image and identity. It is this awareness that enables me to maintain an objective approach in working with a wide variety of people. This awareness has been acquired through many years of dance training and professional work and by dealing with many disturbing as well as delightful personal experiences when learning, performing, teaching and living.

In my opinion, movement and dance are more beneficial when experienced than when being observed or read about. Because you, as a teacher, will be reading about and not experiencing in detail the material covered in a teacher training class, I will review some points that might be helpful.

First I would like to mention what creative modern dance is and why it is the form of dance in which Body Ego Technique has its roots. All dance is somewhat therapeutic and educational. All dance and movement are made up of the same basic elements. As mentioned earlier, creative modern dance has its roots in early childhood movement patterns. Modern dance is a form based on the more natural ways of moving in comparison to the classical ballet form which uses unnatural or more highly conventionalized set positions. It is easier to simplify and separate the elements of modern dance than it is with ballet. Modern dancers do not wear shoes while performing and most other forms of dance require them.

It is important to know about the normal developmental pattern of the first five years of life. It is important to know that there are normal individual variations, especially in timing that can take place during this early development. There are many books such as Gesell's *The First Five Years of Life* that deal specifically with child development.

If you understand the normal growth patterns of a child, it is easier to see minor or gross deviations. If you can see at which stage a child or adult is functioning and if you can understand the developmental relationship as to where he should be chronologically functioning, you have a basis for your class objectives.

All movement, from the beginning of life to the end of life calls upon the same basic skills to carry the movement into effect. These basic movement skills are all learned during these early developmental years. The refinement of these movements are relative to the individual's growth and maturity.

Rhythm, pulse, beat, contract-release, in-out, or up-down are the first visible signs of movement and of life. If you can see these signs, you have a starting point for a class. How large, how small, how fast, how slow, how strong or how weak these movements appear to be are the externalizations of reasons or motivations that cause these movements to be done in this particular way. As the reasons change, the movements change, and as the movements change, so do the reasons or motivations change. For instance, if one is walking along at a slow easy pace, the rhythm would be quite even; the size of the step would be quite even, and the muscle structure would be rather relaxed. The feeling could be one of pleasure. If something frightening should suddenly be seen or heard, the muscles would tighten, the pace or step would become hesitant or irregular and the added tenseness would cause the steps to become smaller and faster. This change in motivation could also cause this same simple walk to develop or suddenly change into a run.

By reversing this action, for instance in a class, you can know that when your student is asked to run across the room, or to walk with short tight steps at a fast tempo, the movements will, indeed, produce a different emotional effect than the one produced by a slow, even and relaxed walk. The emotional and physical *change*, in both instances, take place whether or not the reasons or motivations or the responses are verbally discussed or understood by either teacher or student. As one's physical skills broaden and change, the related emotional experience will broaden and change.

It is important to recognize that the teacher will see visible signs of normal behavior in the most disturbed patient. It is also important to recognize that the teacher will see visible signs of disturbance in the most normal student. It is rare that one is totally disturbed or totally well.

Body Ego Technique and other forms of dancing and physical education are ways to develop movement skills. Body Ego Technique has a broader objective by utilizing these skills for a more total education or re-education of the ego structure. In all of these physical activities, the tool or instrument needed (the body with its total affect) is available for the teacher to see, which can help determine where to begin and how to continue a class. The teacher can also see which of the separate components of movement is most available to be called upon to emphasize, reorganize and coordinate.

In beginning creative modern dance in therapy or in Body Ego Technique, the approach is to use in a variety of ways these separate elements (rhythm, space and force) to gradually organize, coordinate and broaden an individual's movement skills to help create a more balanced behavior. This is not a simple task and it requires a competent, confident, well coordinated and balanced teacher. The teacher must be able to recognize, separate, utilize and reorganize changes in physical body movements and thus, ego states.

The organization of a class structure has been covered in a preceding chapter and detailed class material will be dealt with in a later chapter. However, I would like to make a comparison between what I feel are the needs of all people to the objectives of a class in creative modern dance or Body Ego Technique. We all must find an identity; become aware of our body boundaries; know how much space we use; know how we relate to ourselves and others in space; find our individual timing or rhythm; become aware of the effect that motivation or reason has upon the external expression; and be able to clearly separate fantasy from reality.

The first objective in a class is to become aware that the total body is the expressive tool being used. The boundaries of the body are felt kinesthetically by touching and moving separate parts of the body as well as the coordination of the whole.

The use of space is clarified by moving in various directions, shapes, floor patterns as well as individual, partner and group activities.

Music or drum accompaniment helps one to feel his own timing and also to learn to experience a broad range of rhythms and tempos. The instructor-controlled rhythm and tempo is an important guide line in a class. To effectively beat the drum in relationship to the directed activity is a learned technique and it is not an easy one to learn. Although the teacher does, in general, teach a class at her own most comfortable pace, often the class demands require a different tempo or timing. Unless the instructor is prepared and able to handle this change of timing, she will begin to lose the class.

The final objective is to be able to use this highly trained tool, the body, to nonverbally communicate an idea or thought to someone else. What is expressed can be motivated by a wish, a dream, a hope, a fear, a failure, a success, a rebuttal or a conviction. The desired effect you wish to communicate will determine the amount of force or energy or what quality you use to perform these movements. By "perform" I mean within the class and not performing as done by a professional artist. The performing level of achievement is seldom if ever reached and is not the objective with young children, with beginning students or in a therapy class.

The reality of the class, the environment, the objective directions given, and the limited space and timing, provide a structure in which the student can successfully deal with fantasy or make-believe and can still safely return to his own functioning identity. All too often the objective of a non-professional class is to offer movement to create a physical and emotional release. This is only one step towards the ability to build, explore, direct, vary, broaden and change behavior.

A specific way to vary movement patterns or to create changes of experience is to teach opposites or contrasts of movements. For instance:

In using tempo: fast-slow

Size: big-little, or large-small

Space: circular-straight; wide-narrow

Directions: up-down; high-low; front-back

Shapes: round-angular; bent-straight, etc.

Qualities or ways of moving: smooth-jerky; soft-hard; heavy-light

Reasons or motivations: sadness-happiness; tenderness-meanness; confidence-fright, and of course many others.

By experiencing contrast or opposites, one can recognize how broad his range of movement is and he can feel a personal center point or a balance of his own actions or behavior patterns.

Another way to use movement is to start with a simple movement (if possible, the student's or patient's) and try to *develop* the pattern. By develop, I mean to gradually make the movement wider, larger, smaller, longer, etc. Development can also include growing from the position in space, for instance, from a sitting position with, perhaps a rocking movement to a standing position, still rocking. The standing rocking movement can eventually develop into a turning movement and then perhaps into a locomotor turn. This development should not be threatening to the student. Allow beginners and patients to experience a gradual development; be gentle.

I have found this gentle but positive approach is a most successful one with autistic children. They usually externalize some form of bizarre repetitious movement pattern. Their movements can be developed in many ways, such as changes in shape, size, intensity, tempo, etc. The sudden interruption with contrast or opposites can also be used with these autistic children as with other children, but the instructor should use a little more caution.

In order to understand more clearly and to be able to see at what level your student is functioning, it is necessary to try to relate the visible movements or postures to the possible internal motivations. A person might have a smile on his face, but the amount of tension, flexibility, and the relationship to the other parts of the body, especially to the eyes, will tell you if he is really happy and pleased or if he is shy, afraid and only anxious to please.

A hanging, drooping posture with just enough tenseness to hold it up could indicate that the person is sad and depressed or simply very fatigued. The ability to change and the amount of time involved in this position are the determining factors. When the shoulders are carried high and/or rounded forward, it usually is the result of prolonged fear. However, high tense shoulders accompanied by a forward head and chest could be either a cover-up for insecurity with aggressiveness or it could indicate that the person is determined or angry. The opposite, of course, would be posture that is set with a retracted back and a caved in abdomen and chest. This could be caused by apathy, lethargy, fear or fatigue. The persons with extreme differences in the amount of tension in the various parts of the body are called *split*. For instance, you often see someone who is tense in the upper part of his body and has quite relaxed legs. Perhaps the motivation is continued ambivalence.

The ability to change position, movement and experience and to find a more balanced equilibrium is the ultimate objective in Body Ego Technique. This objective requires enough knowledge about the logical *development* of movement as well as how to use contrasts or opposites in movement.

Even the most literal everyday action such as a gesture can be given a repetitious rhythmic structure. It can be slowed down, quickened, broadened in size, and changed in shape. It can be repeated, continued with the same quality or given a more exaggerated motivation by changes of the various components of movement.

I have found in teaching classes of children, both normal and disturbed, and in teaching classes of disturbed older individuals, that there are certain similarities as well as differences. There is a similarity in concentration span. It is short and the interest is limited. There is a similarity in the emotional fluctuation or instability. The learning process of imitation rather than by verbalization is similar. The need for repetition is similar. The need for simplicity of presentation is similar. A firm but gentle attitude is needed by both groups and they need to establish clear boundary lines to help clarify their sense of identity. A careful selection of terminology (by the instructor) is necessary. One time when I was using a record player for a class of young people in a state hospital, I made the remark, "Do not touch the record player. I just got a shock from it." This unthinking use of the word shock caused great fear among the young people who had literally experienced shock treatment. Another time in a class of normal children around six years of age, a child told her mother than she liked her dancing class but she did not know why I, the teacher, kept saying, "ant hole," When the mother asked me what I meant, I realized that I was saying, "and hold," when I finished a movement and wanted the children to stop. Because they were following my actions and stopped when I did, I was not aware of how meaningless, confusing and unnecessary this verbalization was for this class.

Some of the *differences* I have observed in young children in contrast to older individuals are that: children are just developing and are usually having *new* learning experiences; their reactions are more clear and direct;

they have not built up as many defenses as the adult; their habit patterns are not so set and it is much easier to see the basic feelings being externalized. The adults, especially the disturbed, have strong habit patterns that inhibit their range of movement as well as their ability to change. This makes it difficult for the instructor to perceive, to separate and to work with these set patterns. However, when the older individual learns new movement patterns, his broad background allows for more varied experiences. The more experienced adult who is set or limited, has much to *undo* before his education or ego growth can begin.

The most constant difference between groups of children and adults is the discipline problem. It is rare that adults as a group, even the disturbed, will present much of a discipline problem. It is rare that children, even the most normal, as a group will not present a discipline problem. Sometimes the first objective of communicating to the group can take most of the class period. It is wise to work with small groups or with individuals when the discipline problems interfere with the educational purpose.

In the teacher training class, after the students feel that they understand the theory of Body Ego Technique, they are required to have some teaching experience. I arrange for them to teach some of the normal children's classes and then to accompany me to a hospital and to participate in a therapy class. I would like to end this chapter with some of the remarks made by a few of the students after their first experience with psychiatric patients.

. . . .

. . . The visitation was a good experience in learning about your sensitivity to people and your awareness of movements, yours and others. It is true that there is a very fine line of distinction between the patients and yourself and this became more evident as one works with them. The way they related to us, by looks, words and touch revealed their lack of trust and insecurity about themselves. By watching them move one could begin to actually see their inhibitions, but the most interesting part was what I found out about myself. The sense of being trapped in my own body was the strongest feeling I felt and I recognized the games people play by watching the patients as the class progressed. I would like to follow the visit with similar experiences, the only obstacle being the fear of facing myself.

. . . .

. . . I noted some subtle physical movement limitation by some of the patients, but was more *struck* with the subtlety of differences between 'normal' and 'abnormal.' I feel I do many of the same kinds of things—hesitancy of some movements, resistance to some movements that many patients did, and could not be as spontaneous as others. The fine line between acceptable and desired ego control and satisfaction, and unacceptable or tolerable self is awesomely fragile.

. . . .

. . . My impression of the patients themselves was that they were, as Jeri said, quite limited in their actions and behavior. It was much easier to see this after having discussed it. It also seemed easier when one could think of their behavior and reactions as being predictable. The extremes of behavior are not as frightening if one can see the pattern behind it all. I regret being too occupied to observe body movement more closely—however the physical contact with the patients was very revealing. . . . The contrast between the patients' verbaliza-tions about their actions was a good example of body expression. In the class itself I was surprised at the amount of participation and control on the part of the patients. Even though Jeri was directing the class, it appeared to be more a group effort. Decisions were given to the group or individuals. I believe the class had the feeling they were more in control than they were. . . .

. . . .

. . . I saw the theories we had been discussing come to life, and I saw how effective they could be.

During the course of the evening I saw people who were emotionally "dead" begin to respond; I saw weakened people flex their muscles a bit; slow people quicken; depressed people smile. Although I have included the actual exercises and movements that were used that evening, the novice should beware; nine-tenths of the effectiveness of this "technique" can be attributed to the personality of the "technician." A combination of confidence, compassion, sensitivity, and strength would have to be present in order to deal with these people. The facility with which the instructor handled them belied the degree of expertise involved. . . . A buoyant personality on the instructor's part, along with a show of affec-tion and a certain degree of firmness helped to accomplish this without incident.

. . . .

CHAPTER 9

CLASS TECHNIQUE

Towards the end of each of the teacher training workshop series the students are asked to write about: (1) What they think they have learned in the series of classes. (2) What more they would like to learn about this technique. (3) To make suggestions as to the most useful material they would like to have included in a book on Body Ego Technique.

For the first question one student wrote in part:

> . . . The physical aspects would be difficult to verbalize. I know that I can often change my affective feelings by trying to change my space, or rhythm or my force of movement. . . . communicating to one another is one of the most complex, interesting and necessary things that people do. Complex as it is, everybody can and does do it. From the time we're born, we communicate with our bodies. . . The infant's development occurs in stages including his ability to communicate with his body as well as with his language. The integration of his ability to use space, to use rhythm, to use force and to pattern the combination in a meaningful way come very gradually. . . To be more conscious of the body messages we send to both others and ourselves sometimes takes a great deal more than talking about it, especially with those individuals who are "out of touch" with themselves and/or reality. In class, I believe we progressed from assignments that helped us to be aware of ourselves and how we would go about teaching others these sensitivities about body communication. For example, as an individual, I have a body image of myself. This may or may not hold with how others see me . . . but it is an indication of my own subjective experience of myself at that moment in time. I have weight, muscle tone, posture, and various physical features that make me an individual . . . In addition, I have movement. There are various factors that motivate my movement and together they make up in part my subjective experience of me, and to a lesser extent, the objective experience of me seen by others . . . In order to teach these very simple sensitivities toward one's ego, the parts have to be broken down and exaggerated, and the process has to develop in order from simple to complex, as an infant develops . . . I think the main tool to use to achieve these goals is to change an individual's experience of self. As an instructor, this is the main goal, effect change in an individual . . .

The answers to question two and three seemed to be the same, over and over, in all of the classes. The students all wanted to know more about how to teach specific techniques. In a book, they would like to have these techniques written out in detail.

Based upon this request, the next section of the book is detailed technique. The technique has been broken down into levels of beginning, intermediate and advanced. It is by no means the only way nor does it cover all possibilities. It is designed to provide specific materials with which

132

to work, to show how movement can develop; and to stimulate teachers to vary and change these movements in different ways, as needed for each particular class. The ability of the teacher to be aware of and sensitive to the student's needs will be the determining factor as to how this technique can most effectively be used. There is material that can be used for every or any sort of class.

There are also a few sample classes. These have been included to remind one of the structure of a class and to point out some of the subtle differences in technique in various classes.

Body Awareness—Alignment

1. Awareness of the body is part of the basic foundation of Body Ego Technique. It helps each person become acquainted with his body and the possibilities he has for movement and dance. When a strong and positive image of the body is developed, the range of movement and emotional capabilities increases and a person is better able to achieve a balance within himself. Awareness of the body and alignment are stressed throughout the class. Alignment of the parts of the body means that the parts should be equally balanced on both vertical halves of the central axis and that horizontally the parts should be balanced front and back and side to side.

2. Look in a mirror and observe your own alignment. Which parts of your body are out of alignment? Can you exaggerate the position of your head; shoulders; hips; feet; tilt? Do this from both a front view and a side view.

3. Think of the body and all of its parts. Which ones can move?
   a. Head
   b. Neck
   c. Shoulders
   d. Ribs
   e. Back
   f. Arms
   g. Elbows
   h. Hands
   i. Wrists
   j. Fingers
   k. Abdominals
   l. Waist
   m. Pelvis
   n. Hips
   o. Legs
   p. Thighs
   q. Knees
   r. Feet
   s. Toes

4. How many ways can each part move?
   a. Bending
   b. Rotating
   c. Twisting
   d. Circling-turning
   e. Dropping
   f. Opening-closing
   g. Shaking
   h. Swinging
   i. Extending
   j. Contracting
   k. Relaxing
5. Move each part of the body separately.
6. Move various body parts in combination.
7. Align the body correctly. There should be equal lift and drop of both the front and back of the body. There should be equal distribution on each side of an imaginary vertical line.
8. Take exaggerated shapes and postures to show different ways of feeling:
   a. *Anger*—clenched fists, shoulders lifted, head forward, elbows bent in contraction, body in forward tilt, exaggerated tension.
   b. *Sadness*—head and shoulders drooped, back rounded, very little energy in arms and legs.
   c. *Happiness*—Head up, chest area open, shoulders back, lifted quality throughout the body, feet slightly turned out.
   d. *Fearfulness*—Head held back, shoulders raised and rounded inward, feet and legs turned inward, hips either held in an exaggerated way under and downward or tilted upward and out; body is tilted back; parts of the body are made to look as small as possible.
   e. *Silliness*—Usually a cover-up for another emotion. All body parts are held and positioned in an exaggerated and awkward manner.

Beginning

1. Label verbally and rhythmically each body part.
2. Touch each part separately and in a continuous rhythm, e.g.,
   Touch your head, head, head;
   Touch your shoulders, shoulders, shoulders;
   Touch your knees, knees, knees;
   Touch your toes, toes, toes.
3. Allow each student to originate movement in each part, e.g.,
   Move your head; move your arms; etc.
4. Ask different members of the class to originate movement for a particular part of the body. All follow the movement, e.g.,
   "Dave, show us a way to move your hips."
5. Move and coordinate two body parts together, such as legs and arms or

hips and head. Either allow each to originate his own movement to a particular count or rhythm or all follow someone in the class.

6. Present a sequence such as:
   Move your arms. Hold.
   Move your head. Hold.
   Move your hips. Hold.
   Move your legs. Hold.
   Move everything at once. Hold.
   Use tempo changes.

7. Present a sequence in which movement is successive, such as:
   Shake your head. Add your shoulders. Add your arms. Add your hips. Add your legs. Shake everything. Turn around. Hold. Repeat. Do the sequence in various tempos.

8. Move each part of the body in a specific way, rhythmically, e.g.,
   Move your head *up* and *down;* up and down; up and down.

9. Sitting or standing. Each person in the circle runs individually around the outside of the circle, touching each member of the group on the shoulders. Note individual differences as each touches.

Intermediate

1. Create *set patterns* for each part of the body to move in isolation, eg., a specific movement or group of movements for each part.

2. Allow each person to originate his own pattern of movement within a set rhythm, e.g.,
   Take 4 counts to move each of the following parts separately:
   head; shoulders; arms; hips; legs (separately)
   Combine all the parts moving together for 8 counts.
   Repeat the entire sequence. Vary the direction person is facing and also the tempo.

3. Align each part of the body together into a total coordinated unit. See *definition of alignment.*

4. Give a particular rhythm or quality for each person to move to. Use a verbal suggestion, drum, piano or record, e.g.,
   Clap a rhythm and move a part of the body to that rhythm or suggest a feeling or tempo to move each part separately and in combination.

5. Move through space in any locomotor activity, such as a walk or skip. Add the body moving in various ways as the person is walking or skipping, e.g.,
   Walk and move your head side to side 4 times;
   Walk and reach with arms out and in 4 times;
   Walk, moving hips side and side 4 times;
   Repeat the pattern.

6. Moving through space, move the body parts in syncopation or opposition, e.g.,
   Walking very fast, move the arms very slowly.

7. Mirror a partner's movements and use specific parts of the body as limitations. Follow your partner's head movements. Then head and arms, etc. Limitations, such as direction (movements which only go up and down) or tempo (speed).

Advanced

1. Align each part of the body together into a total coordinated unit. See *definition of alignment.*
2. Use a particular body part to initiate a specific movement such as a fall or turn or walk, eg.,
   Push your hip to the side as far as you can until you go into an off-balanced position, letting the hip lead you into a turn. Descend to the floor leading with your right shoulder.
   Move across the floor leading with your head.
3. Lean your body from the ankles into an off-balanced position. When the point of balance is lost, take the motion into a specific movement such as a run or fall or turn. Explore balance and lead into off-balanced positions with various body parts.
4. Allow the class to create specific combinations with emphasis on body parts. Vary the quality of movements from sharp, percussive to smooth, sustained.
5. Walk with exaggerated parts of the body such as: forward head, lifted shoulders and arms, hips back and feet turned out.
6. Choose a particular feeling and allow the feeling to cause the various exaggerated postures and tempos and rhythms.

Warm-ups

The purpose of warm-ups is to literally warm the muscles of the body so that they are more flexible and better prepared to stretch and perform at the will of the dancer. Warm-ups should always precede any stretches and contractions. This will help prevent torn muscles or spasms and allow the circulation to increase and prepare the body for more exaggerated physical action.

Warm-up technique can be done with isolated parts of the body or the body moving as a total unit. Good warming-up actions would include swinging, bouncing and shaking movements or combinations of these. It should be noted that swinging motions are the most effective way to prepare the body for dance. The following are examples of swings for various parts of the body and developments of the swing from beginning through advanced. The main difference between material for the disturbed or beginning student as compared to the advanced or professional dancer is one of style, refinement, rhythms, and development of the material. Many of the beginning movement ideas will be similar for the advanced student, and equally as valuable; only the emphasis and technical ability will differ.

Beginning

1. *Circle formation.* Note: when teaching swings, emphasize the *drop-lift* quality.
   a. Have the class hold hands or stand separately. Lead them in swinging motions of the head, arms, legs, torso, hips, etc.
   b. Have the class shake the various parts of the body. Add all the parts of the body together and shake as a total unit. Repeat the sequence.
2. Arms swing front and back several times. Add the knees bending in a down-up action each time the arms go front and back.
   Arms swing front: knees down-up
   Arms swing back: knees down-up
3. *Circle formation.* All hold hands and balance on left foot, swing the right leg forward and backward several times. Repeat on the opposite leg. This can be done to a specific count or not, eg.,
   Swing the right leg—8 counts.
   Swing the left leg—8 counts.
   Repeat.
4. Swing the head side to side several times to get the swing action.
5. Swing the arms side to side, first going the same direction, then opposing each other in an in-out pattern.
6. Name a particular part of the body and ask different people in the class to swing that part in any way they want. All follow, eg.,
   Show us a way to swing your torso. All pick up the motion and rhythm and follow.

Intermediate

Put the swings into various combinations with set counts and rhythms. Swings usually move best in 3/4 or 6/8 meter.
1. At barre or in center floor:

a. Swing *head* toward barre and away 4 times (side to side).

b. Add the outside arm in the same swinging motion, drop across the body, lift to overhead position and out to the side again 4 times.

c. Extend the outside arm over the head, in toward the barre and out 4 times (body curves side to side). More of a sway or rock action.

d. Push the hip toward the barre and out 4 times.
e. Do each of the above (a–d) separately and then in combination.

2. Holding the barre with the right hand (or center floor with both arms in open position).
   a. Do 8 leg swings forward and backward, swinging from the hip. Turn the body in toward the barre and around to face opposite direction with left hand on barre (count 8 and). Repeat 8 leg swings forward and backward, turning in toward the barre and ending in the original position.

b. Do 8 leg swings with the leg lifted to the side and closing the hip to swing toward the barre and opening the hip across the body (in and out). Turn to the opposite direction on count 8 *and.* Then repeat side leg swings, turning on count 8 *and,* finishing in original direction and position.
3. *Center floor swing combinations:* these can be done for warm-ups, but might best be put in the section of the class called "center floor." These are developments of the swings used at barre.

a. Body in second position (feet open and turned out). Bounce the knees up and down. Add the arms in a swinging motion, across the body and out. (Knees bounce up and down to each arm motion.)
1. Swing the arms across the body, then stretch them over to frame head to the side, alternating sides of the body each time. (Bounce and stretch to side—count 1 and stretch counts 2, 3, 4.)

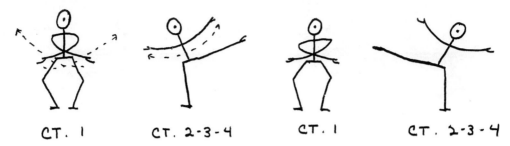

CT. 1   CT. 2-3-4   CT. 1   CT. 2-3-4

2. Repeat *a* but take weight onto one leg and balance with the other leg lifted to the side. (Bounce and balance.) Count 1-bounce and counts 2, 3, 4 balance. Alternate sides.
3. Swing across the body and turn one-half turn on the outward motion. (Swing and turn.) Count 1 and 2, 3, 4. Meter can be 3/4 also.

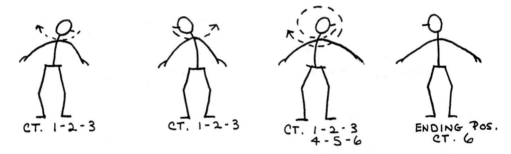

CT. 1-2-3   CT. 1-2-3   CT. 1-2-3 4-5-6   ENDING POS. CT. 6

b. *Half circle–full circle and a half combination:* this is done in 6/8 meter. First the head moves in isolation, the arms and upper torso are added to the action. This is repeated again with the knees bending and allowing the entire torso to move in one motion and concluding in a side fall.
1. Directions are given for the right side and should be reversed for the left side.
2. Person standing in an open leg or second position, head is turned to the right side of the body. Head swings to the left in isolation (count 1, 2, 3)—half circle: head swings back through the same path to the right (count 4, 5, 6); head then swings to the left and continues in a full circle and a half, ending with head facing the left, counts 1, 2, 3, 4, 5, 6. Repeat the entire sequence beginning left. (2 measures of 6–8).

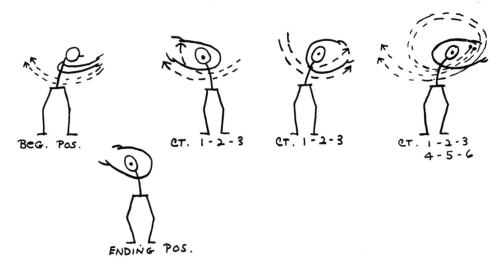

BEG. POS.   CT. 1-2-3   CT. 1-2-3   CT. 1-2-3
                                        4-5-6

ENDING POS.

3. Repeat the above sequence b-2 adding the upper torso and arms to the head movement. Make sure that the arms come to the overhead position and frame the head and they hold the body in a lateral tipped diagonal line. Repeat to other direction.

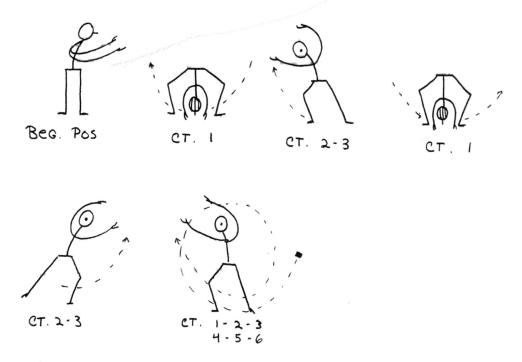

BEG. POS   CT. 1   CT. 2-3   CT. 1

CT. 2-3   CT. 1-2-3
                4-5-6

4. Repeat the same sequence adding the knees and entire torso, ending in a side fall to the right after the last circle and a half.

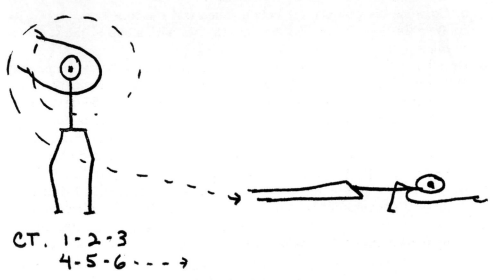

CT. 1-2-3
   4-5-6----→

5. Repeat the entire sequence beginning to the left and ending in a side fall to the left. See explanation of side fall, pages 148 and 157.

Advanced

1. Combine the front and back leg swings with the side leg swings, changing directions without stopping.
2. After doing the Intermediate Swing combination (Drawings 1–4) add the side fall, torso and outside arm reaching in toward the barre, outside hip pulling out (away from barre) 6 counts to fall. Repeat on other side.

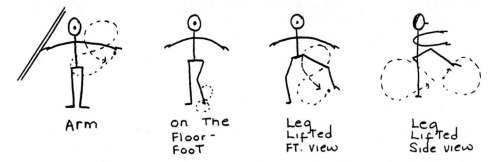

Arm   on The   Leg   Leg
             Floor-   Lifted   Lifted
             FooT   FT. View   Side view

3. *Figure 8 swings:* Each part is taught separately and put into a combination in 3/4 or 6/8 meter.
   a. At barre or center floor. Cross the outside arm in front of the body, forming a circle, then complete the figure 8 by circling the arm in toward the body in back (*front circle, back circle*). Repeat in a continuous pattern.
   b. Describe the same pattern with the outside foot on the floor. (Front circle, back circle). Repeat.

    c. Lift the leg so it is bent at the knee. Repeat the figure 8 pattern with the leg in the air.

    d. Combine the arm and leg action. Then add the torso.

    e. Take the figure 8 combination into the air, with a hop of the supporting leg on count 1 and 4.

4. Developments of swings and other technique covered in the beginning of the class can be presented later in class as progressions across the floor.

    a. Combine 3-d and 3-e in a progression moving across the floor, using both arms in the same figure 8 action on opposite sides of the body.

    b. Take swings to each side in a progression across the floor. First do the swings in a very slow tempo with a heavy quality; then do the same swing in a fast tempo, taking the uplift off the floor.

5. Have the class create various swing progressions changing the tempo, quality, direction, floor pattern, or motivation. Have the class learn to do each combination. Combine several of their swing ideas into an extended combination or development.

Preparatory Techniques

After the body is warm, technique that strengthens and extends its range of possibilities should follow. These activities should include:

1. points and brushes with the feet
2. leg lifts
3. pliés (knee bends)
4. relevés (raising to the ball of the foot)
5. hinges or thigh and back strengthening
6. contractions and extensions of all parts of the body
7. stretches of all parts of the body
8. preparations for jumps, leaps, hops, turns
9. preparations for falls and ways to lift the body from a fall
10. preparation for any other material to be covered in a more developed form later in the class

Correct alignment and positioning of the body and the relationship of its parts should be emphasized during the technique section of the class. Proper landing and takeoff for aerial actions should also be emphasized.

The technique section will be divided into four categories rather than in groupings of beginning, intermediate and advanced. The technique does not vary greatly from beginning to advanced, for technique is a form of drill to perfect the body. The developments and amounts of material that should be covered in a class will be determined by the age and ability of your students. The categories will be as follows:

1. Techniques for building strength
2. Techniques for increasing flexibility
3. Preparations for jumps, hops, leaps and turns
4. Preparation for falls and lifts

Techniques for Building Strength—at barre

1. *Feet:* for the beginning student, have them brush and extend the foot forward, sideward, backward. Touch or point the foot each direction 4 times. Change sides and repeat with the other foot. Use the outside foot (away from barre).

2. *Feet:* keeping both legs straight, brush the outside foot along the floor and into a point (leg and foot are turned out). The starting position is with the heels together and feet turned out (first position). Brush forward—4 counts.
   Pull the foot back into position—4 counts.
   Repeat 3 times.
   Brush to the side—4 counts.
   Pull the foot back into position—4 counts.
   Repeat 3 times.
   Brush to the back—4 counts.
   Pull the foot back into position—4 counts.
   Repeat 3 times.
   Repeat to the side position 4 times.
   a. Repeat the above sequence—brushes forward, side back, side—using 1 count out and 1 count in. Do 4 times each direction.
   b. Repeat the above sequence using only 1 count to move the foot both out and in. It would be counted (out-in)—and 1—and 2—and 3—and 4. This should be done with intermediate and advanced students, as it is difficult to correctly move the foot (flex and extend the ankle) so rapidly.

BRUSH FWD. FLEX-   ROTATE   DRAW
4 CTS.   EXTEND   EACH   FT. BACK
            FOOT   DIRECTION   TO POS.

3. *Feet:* repeat number 2, brushing the foot out 4 counts and in 4 counts. Add to that the following:
   Brush out 4 counts.
   Flex and extend the foot for 4 counts.
   Rotate the foot at the ankle outward for 4 counts.
   Rotate the foot at the ankle inward for 4 counts.
   Return the foot to the original position (brushing it along the ground) —4 counts.

POINT   LIFT Leg   POINT

4. *Feet:* Brush the foot to a point—count 1.
   Lift the leg, without bending the knee or back—count 2.
   Return to a point—count 3.
   Draw the foot back to original position—count 4.
   Repeat the above 4 times in each direction—forward, sideward, backward, sideward.

FRONT   SIDE   BACK

5. *Leg Lifts:* brush the foot through the pointed position and extend it off the floor, lifting the leg. Do this in one motion. Do 4 leg lifts to each direction, keeping a good turnout. Repeat on the other side.

   Note: Make sure in all the above techniques that the standing leg is straight and that the ankles of both feet do not roll inward. Hips should be under and upper body is not tense. The outside arm can be held at the side or curved at chest height to the side.

6. *Pelvic Tilt:* Have the students stand with their side to the barre. Work on tilting the pelvis, in isolation, forward and backward (out, in, back and under). This should be done in every class by all levels of ability, for it helps balance the strength and flexibility of the back and abdominal muscles and is involved in all movement.

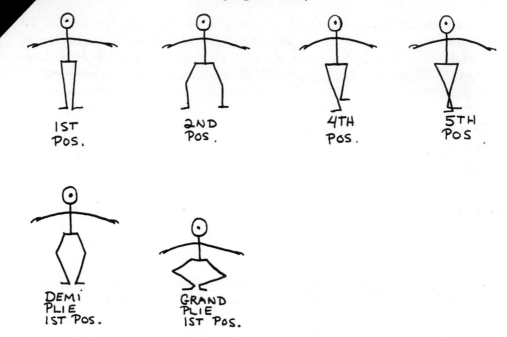

7. *Ankles and thighs:* Pliés or knee bends can be done in several different traditional positions—1st, 2nd, 4th and 5th, e.g.,
   1st position (heels together and feet turned out). Do two pliés keeping the heels on the ground. Go down as far as possible without tilting the hips out or leaning the back forward. The hips sink evenly down between bent knees. Do this 2 counts down and 2 counts up.
   Repeat 3 times. (demi-pliés)
   Extend the plié until the heels come off the ground and the body lowers as far as possible without leaning or collapsing. Knees remain open and turned out. Take 4 counts down and 4 counts up. Repeat. Change directions and repeat.

8. *Thighs, back and abdomen. Hinges.* Feet are parallel. Bend the knees, keeping the hips under (as if standing), tilt the torso backward in one unit from the knees, deepen the bend at the ankles and knees. Keep the body in a straight line with the knees and continue as far as possible without arching the back or collapsing the knees. Increase the hinge

until the student can extend all the way to the floor, resting on the shoulders, and up again through the same movement. Set a number of counts for hinging down and up, such as 4 counts, then 8 counts. After this is learned at the barre, have the class repeat the hinge in center floor.

T - HINGE .

a. Repeat the hinge going only halfway, so that the torso is horizontal to the ground. When this position is achieved, lift the right or left leg to the front so that the torso and legs form a T. It should be noted that this development is an advanced technique. Take into locomotor turn.

9. *Thighs and torso:* Face the barre, holding the lower barre with both hands. Squat down—count 1.
   Push the thighs in toward the barre and arch the back as the body begins to rise—count 2.
   Continue the pushing motion of the thighs and roll the torso forward from the arch, ending in a stand—count 3.
   Repeat the action several times.
   Face away from the barre and repeat without support.

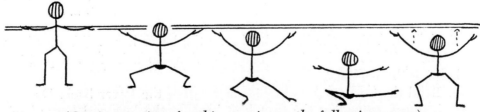

(See instructions for this exercise on the following page.)

10. *Legs:* face the barre in 2nd position (legs wide and turned out).
    Do a deep plie to the floor—count 1.
    Sit on the left heel, right leg straighten—count 2.
    Sit behind the left heel, touching the hip to floor—count 3.
    Pull the body up to a stand, moving through second position—count 4.
    Repeat to the other side.
    Repeat, facing away from the barre, without support.
    It should be noted that this is an advanced technique.
11. For increased strength of the legs and ankles, the brushes and leg lifts
    can be done while standing on half-toe (relevé).

Techniques for Extending Flexibility

1. *Side torso stretch:* Right side to the barre, hold barre with right hand.
   Extend the left arm to the side. Reach the left arm in an arc to position
   directly overhead—1, 2, 3. Extend the left arm in an arc over the head
   and in toward the barre, without twisting the torso—4, 5, 6. Bring the
   arm back to overhead position—1, 2, 3. Reach the left arm to the side
   and lean toward that side (left side)—4, 5, 6.
   Repeat several times.
   Repeat on the other side.
   This is the beginning of the lead-up for the side fall. Refer to *side-fall.*

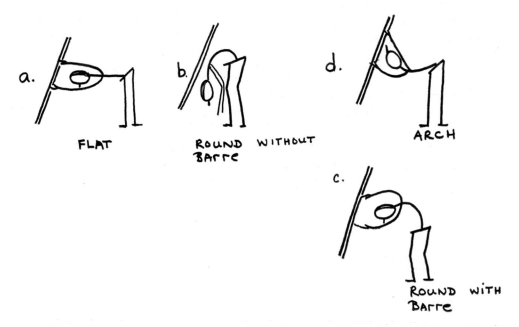

a.   FLAT

b.   ROUND WITHOUT BArrc

d.   ARCH

c.   ROUND WITH BArrc

2. *Back stretch:* Face the barre, hold onto the lower barre. If center floor,
   extend arms above head and bend the body to a horizontal position,
   keeping the back flat.
   a. Bend the torso at the hip joint and flatten the lower back. Do easy
      bounces, extending the stretch at back of the legs and lower back.

b. Round the back, head dropped forward. Let go of the barre and stretch to the floor, keeping the knees straight. Do easy bounces in this position.

c. Combine the flat back stretch with the round back stretch. 8 counts each position.

d. Holding onto the lower barre, back starting in a flat back position. Arch the torso and neck—count 1 and stretch in this position—2, 3, 4. Round the torso—count 1 and stretch in this position—count 2, 3, 4. Repeat the above in 2 counts each position.
Repeat the above in 1 count each position.

3. *Lower leg:* Face the barre, bend the right knee and place it front. Keep the left leg straight and in parallel position. Lean the body weight onto the forward leg and stretch the back leg by pushing the heel toward the floor in an easy bouncing motion. Do 8 times on the left leg and change to the right leg—8 counts.

4. *Thigh:* Inside and back. Facing the barre, extend the right leg over the top or bottom barre. Keep supporting leg and hip close to the barre (depending on height and flexibility).

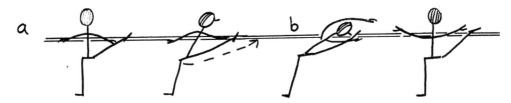

a. Standing leg and leg over the barre in open hip position, ease the leg on the barre further out, increasing the inside stretch of the thigh. Out 4 counts and back up to original position—4 counts. Do two or more times.

b. Standing leg out a few inches from the barre. Torso facing the leg over the barre, arm on same side as leg over the barre is held overhead. Extend the torso and arm out and down to touch the head to the raised (stretched on barre) leg—count 1, 2; lift the torso to the original position—count 3. Repeat several times.
Repeat with the other leg.

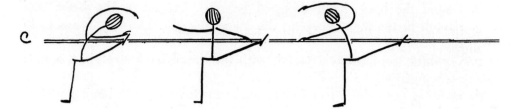

c. Standing leg straight down from the barre, hip touching the barre. Leg over the barre is straight and turned out. Opposite arm is extended overhead. Opposite arm reaches over the head and touches the raised leg, allowing for a good side-torso stretch and leg stretch combined. Reach over the head—count 1, 2, 3 and other arm stretches overhead to the opposite side—count 1, 2, 3. eg.,

Left arm reaches over the head and toward the right lifted leg— 3 counts.

Right arm reaches over the head and toward the left side—3 counts.

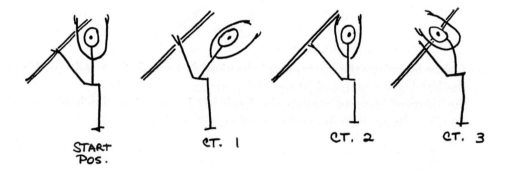

START POS.   CT. 1   CT. 2   CT. 3

CT. 4

5. *Thigh and torso:* Side to the barre, holding barre with right hand, right leg extended over the barre. Extend both arms above the head. Extend the arms and torso, as a total unit to the left side (away from the barre) —count 1.

Lift the torso and arms to center position (upright)—count 2.

Bend the arms and torso to the right (in toward the barre)—count 3.

Lift the torso and arms to center position (upright)—count 4.
Repeat several times. Change sides. Intermediate and advanced technique.

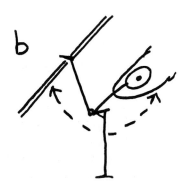

a. Same as above except extend the outward position of the arms and torso even further, then drop the arms, head and torso front, lifting them as a unit in toward the barre. Take this circular action into a *whip swing* quality. Make sure that the lifted leg is held straight, turned out and placed firmly on the barre. It should be noted that this is an advanced technique. When given a swing quality, the count should be changed to 3/4 meter.

b. The same action as above except that the swing of the torso moves from side to side instead of circling around.

6. *Stretch for splits* (inside of thighs): Face away from the barre, extend one leg ahead of the other, both feet turned out. Continue to slide the front leg forward and lower the body to the ground as both arms extend to either side to hold weight and aid in controlling the stretch. Work the body down as far as possible, holding the position without straining. Then roll the body to the side and slowly bring the legs together; stand and repeat with the other leg in front. Not for beginners.

PREPARATIONS FOR JUMPS, HOPS, LEAPS AND TURNS

It is very valuable to work on specific skills involved in jumps, hops, leaps and turns. It is important to align the body properly and to build up strength to properly execute these techniques. This can be done at barre or holding onto a wall or in center floor. The following are suggestions for establishing both the correct position of the body and teaching the correct action involved in performing the specific skill.

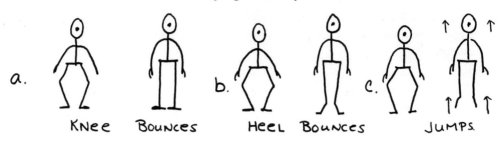

a.   Knee Bounces   b.   Heel Bounces   c.   Jumps.

Jumps

1. Take a position standing with the heels together, toes turned out, arches lifted, toes firmly gripping the floor, and hips held under. Bounce the knees 8 times (demi-plié), making sure knees open out. Bounce the heels off the ground, extending the knees 8 times. This action begins with a knee bend (plié) and goes to half-point and is continuous. Take the bouncing action off the floor and into jumps 8 times.
   a. 8 knee bounces
   b. 8 bounces and lift to half point (heel bounces)
   c. 8 jumps
   Make sure that the preparation and landing positions are with a bent knee (plié). This gives the necessary impetus to get off the ground and allows the body to absorb the shock when landing. The feet go through an extended push-off into pointed feet when in the air (long feet).
2. Practice jumps in place, using a rhythmic pattern and stressing correct placement and action.
   a. Have each person do a set of 8 jumps alone, progressing from one person to another without stopping. They must be prepared to start and finish on time.
   b. Have each person do a set of 16 jumps, progressing from one person to another without stopping. The first 8 must be straight jumps, the second 8 can be their own jumping variations.
   c. Jumping in a changing rhythmic pattern. See the beginning rhythm section number 17.

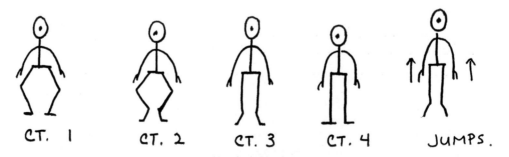

Ct. 1   Ct. 2   Ct. 3   Ct. 4   Jumps.

3. A good strength and placement technique for intermediate and advanced students is the following:

Take a position with the heels together, toes turned out, arches lifted, and toes firmly gripping the floor, hips held under.

a. Bend the knees in plié on count 1.

b. Push the feet to half-point while still in plié—count 2.

c. Extend the knees to a straight position while still on half-toe—count 3.

d. Lower the heels to the ground with knees still straight—count 4. Repeat several times at a slow tempo. Increase the tempo until the action can be taken off the ground into a jump.

e. The above action can also be reversed.

4. The above jump preparations can also be done with the feet apart (second position); either foot in front of the other in closed or open position (fourth or fifth positions).

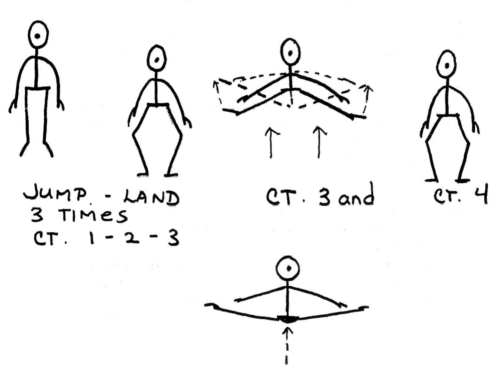

JUMP - LAND
3 TIMES
CT. 1 - 2 - 3

CT. 3 and

CT. 4

5. Preparation for the *Spread-jump Combination:* Holding onto the barre or center floor, do three straight jumps with heels together and toes turned out—counts 1, 2, 3. Jump, opening the legs to the side and forward (sitting in the air with legs apart)—and 4. To make sure the position in the air is clear, have the class sit on the floor in a wide stride position with arms extended over the legs.

Hops and Skips

It is necessary for a person to have the strength and coordination to hop on each leg before he will be able to skip.

1. Facing the barre, hop on each foot separately several times.
2. Hop on each foot separately several times without holding onto the barre. Emphasize the same pushing action used in the jump.
3. Skip a set number of times on each foot. e.g., Hop 4 times on the right leg and 4 times on the left leg. Repeat, with 2 hops on each leg. Do this with or without the barre. Emphasize the lift of each knee.
4. Have each person individually or with group take the 2 count hop (2 hops on each leg) and move it through space, speeding the tempo and emphasizing the alternating lift of each knee. When this is done, the combined hops become a basic skip.

CT. 1   CT. 1-and   CT. 2   CT. 2-and

5. Facing the barre or center floor, prepare the class for the *skip-turn*. This turn is difficult for young children.
   a. Feet are both turned outward for better control and balance.
   Step forward with the right foot.
   Hop on the right foot, lifting the left thigh out and back (leg is bent at the knee, foot is pointed)—count 1 and.
   Step backward with the left foot—count 2.
   Hop on the left foot, lifting the right thigh out and forward (leg is bent at the knee, foot is pointed)—count 2 and.
   Repeat this action several times on the right side, then reverse sides.

CT. 1   CT. 2   CT. 3   CT. 4

Leaps

1. Face slightly to the barre, heels together and toes turned out.
   a. Lift the left leg forward—count 1.
   b. Leap onto the left leg (push off from right leg and land on left—

count 2. Remain in a plie position, right leg now lifted back and straight.

   c. Step back onto the right foot—count 3.

   d. Close the left foot to the right as in original position—count 4.

   e. Repeat several times, then change sides.

2. Repeat number 1 increasing the tempo. Work for length of reach rather than height. Emphasize the correct preparation for push-off and landing, as discussed in the preparation for jumps.

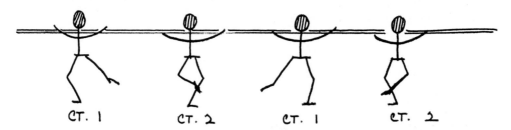

CT. 1   CT. 2   CT. 1   CT. 2

3. Face the barre, both hands holding the barre, or in center floor. Start with heels together and toes turned out (first position).

   a. Lift the right leg to the right side—count 1.

   b. Push off from the left leg onto the right, landing in plie—count 2. Bring the left foot behind the right knee or ankle (side leap).

   c. Extend the left leg to the left side; push off from the right foot and land on the left leg, landing in plie—count 1, 2 (side leap).

   d. Repeat the side leaps several times. Alter the tempo from slow to fast.

Turns

1. Do all of the technique at barre, turning from one side to the other. This motion becomes a *half-turn,* turning the body in toward the barre each time.

2. Teach spotting (focusing on a spot at eye level) while doing technique which requires balance. This is involved in turns such as the *spin-turn.* Some turns are done without one central focus; this requires several points of focus or a revolving focus in which the eyes can focus on a path around the body as it turns.

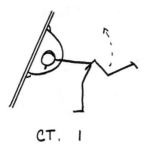

CT. 1

CT. 2.

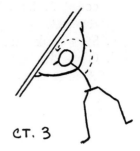

CT. 3

CT. 3 - END

CT. 4

3. *Hip Turn* (center floor turn, lead up to T turn or hip turn locomotor progression):
   a. Face the barre, hold the lower barre, bend body forward at the hip. The leg in the air is bent when action starts.
   b. Moving to the right: lift the left thigh back, continuing the action pivoting to the right side. As this occurs, open both hip joints fully and let the left hip roll over with the thigh until the body is facing back in a modified hinge position (both feet on ground, on half toe, body leaning back in a diagonal position from the ankle and hip, arms overhead and reversing their original grip). Take 3 counts to complete this total action. Reverse the path and repeat. Change sides.
   c. Repeat the above, except take the action completely over and continue another hip roll turn in the same direction, progressing down the barre. Repeat on other side.

CT. 1 CT. 2 CT. 3 CT. 4

CT. 5 CT. 6.

PREPARATION FOR FALLS AND LIFTS

1. *Side Fall:* Side to the barre, feet parallel, outside arm lifted to side.
   a. Lift the outside arm over the head and in towards the barre. This action is then reversed so that the arm lifts overhead and extends outward. Do this action in slow 3/4 meter tempo and then in 6/8 meter.
   b. Add an exaggerated motion of the hips moving in toward the barre and out as the arm moves overhead. As the arm moves in, the hips move away from the barre and vice versa.
   c. Add to the above the deep bending of the knees (bending forward). The knees bend when the arm reaches in toward the barre and straighten as the arm is carried away from the barre.
   d. Take 6 slow counts to take the arm overhead and reach in toward the barre, deepening the knee bend, extending the hips away from the barre. Continue to reach in toward the barre with the arms and away from the barre with the hips while the knees lower the body close to the ground—count 5.

      Sit on the floor with the hips and let the torso extend out into the floor, allowing the arms to also circle down and out until the body is fully extended on the floor sideways—count 6. The last action is very rapid and smooth in order to allow the body to roll into the fall.
   e. To rise from this fall, lift the top hip and rib cage bringing the body to a sitting position. Immediately keep the action going (impetus) by folding the inside leg inward and crossing the outside leg over the inside thigh, pulling the body upward in a diagonal direction.
   f. Repeat d and e varying the number of counts from 6 counts to 4 counts to 2 counts to 1 count. Alternate sides in between counts or do the change of counts on each side separately.
   g. After this fall is learned, have the students come up to the toes on count 1 and give a larger lift and impetus to the fall.

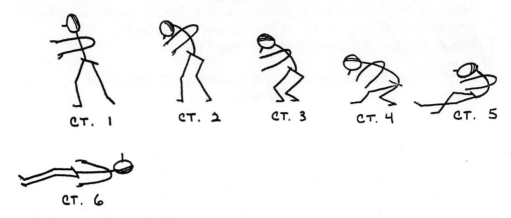

CT. 1   CT. 2   CT. 3   CT. 4   CT. 5

CT. 6

2. *Back Fall:* Face the barre, both hands holding the lower barre.
   a. Step backward with the right foot, rounding the body forward as you
      do so. Let the body roll backward as the back leg bends. The hips
      lead the body and the torso is held forward until the hips touch the
      ground. At this point the torso continues the action by rolling back-
      ward and finishing with the back on the ground.
   b. To rise from the back fall, reverse the above action. Make sure the
      action begins with the head, continues through the spine, taking the
      body weight forward and into the legs. The action should be smooth
      and continuous.
   c. Repeat a and b on the other side, using the other leg. A variation
      could have the back leg turn out and bend in toward the body, letting
      the hips sit behind the leg. This position would also be used to ride,
      with the hips lifting over the leg.
   d. Add a hop on the forward leg and have it continue into the fall.
   e. Pull on the barre with both hands, reaching backward with the hips,
      let go of the barre and let the hips pull you into an off-balanced posi-
      tion forcing a short run and ending in the back fall.
3. Combine the *back fall* and the *side fall* together:
   a. Right side to the barre; do the side fall in 6 counts; as you come up,
      face the barre.
   b. Use the right leg to take you into the back fall—6 counts; end with
      left side facing the barre.
   c. Repeat the side fall in this direction—6 counts, ending up facing the
      barre.
   d. Repeat the back fall, using the left leg to lead into it.
   e. Repeat a through d, changing the counts from 4 to 2 to 1.
4. *Hinge Fall* (advanced): See *techniques for building strength.*
5. While at the barre, give the class a specific number of counts and have
   them develop a method of falling or descending to the floor and rising
   within the set number of counts.
6. Designate a particular body part or direction and challenge the class to

develop a method of falling and rising within that limitation. e.g., Fall to a forward direction. Find a way of turning to the floor.

7. Use an emotional motivation to develop falls.

Basic Technique and Combinations for Center Floor
Stretches

a.  b.

1. Standing position, feet parallel at hip width, shoulders held down:
   a. Raise the arms above the head, increasing the height of one arm, then the other (stretching one side of torso, then the other), weight is raised to half-toe position and hips are held under—8 counts.
   b. Round the arms forward, and begin to round the head, neck, shoulders, upper back, middle back, lower back until the torso is rounded completely forward and the legs are held straight—8 counts.
   c. Allow the body to hang relaxed in this position—8 counts.
   d. Uncurl the torso to a straight, upright position (vertebra by vertebra, beginning in the lower back and ending with the head)—8 counts.
   e. Repeat a through d several times.

a.  b.

e

(See instructions for this exercise on the following page.)

2. Standing position, feet in a wide turned out position (second position), hips held under, shoulders down.

     a. Reach the right arm overhead, left arm straight down and sliding along the left leg. Extend the right arm from a position straight in the air to a motion which takes it in a stretch overhead and to the left side. Keep the arm close to the ear and straight at the elbow— 4 counts.

     b. Stretch the right arm, while in the extended overhead position, making sure that the torso remains facing forward—4 counts.

     c. Repeat a and b using the left arm.

     d. Continue to alternate right and left arms several times.

     e. A more advanced technique is to repeat the above, reaching both arms simultaneously to each side without decreasing the stretch, but placing more control in the abdominal area.

3. Standing position, feet parallel. Bend the back forward and touch the head to the knees. Bend both knees and straighten them as tight as possible, keeping the head firmly in place. This is to stretch the back of the legs.

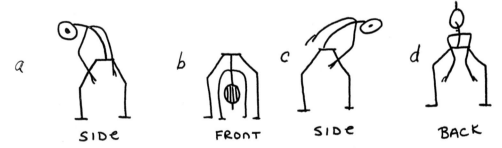

4. Standing stretches in all directions—feet in an open position (second); hips held under and shoulders down.

     a. Bend body-side-front-side-back. Start front—8 bouncing motions each direction, right-front-left-back (1–4).

     b. Let the torso rotate to the front, back rounded and arms rounded down—8 bouncing motions to the front.

     c. Take left arm and extend it overhead to the right, keeping the body front—8 bouncing motions to the side (right side).

d. Rotate the torso back and let the arms and head fall back as well; hips are still under and the motion is in the knees and ankles as well.

e. Repeat a through d reversing directions each time through a complete set.

f. Repeat e and alter the counts for each set: 8 counts; 4 counts; 2 counts; 1 count.

5. Sitting, put the soles of the feet together and hold onto each ankle simultaneously, elbows pressing on the inside of the knees. First with a flat back and then with a round back, lean the torso forward and press the knees to the floor—8 counts each.

6. Sitting, legs together and straight in front of the torso. Stretch the arms forward over the legs, first with a flat back, then with a rounded back —8 counts each.

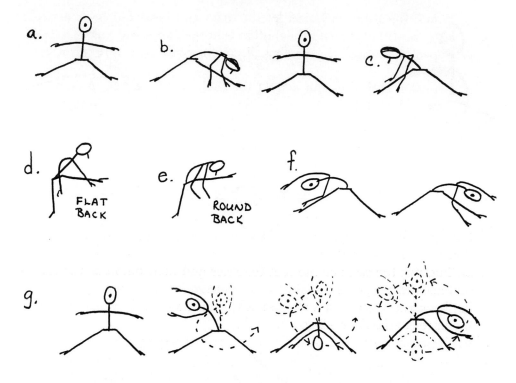

7. Sitting, legs spread apart in an open position, legs and feet turned out from the hip joint.
   a. Lean the torso forward between the legs with the back flat, pressing the pelvis *through* the legs and forward. Hands may be placed on the floor or extended forward in space—8 counts.
   b. Reach the arms and turn the torso over the right leg and stretch—8 counts.
   c. Reach the arms and turn the torso over the left leg and stretch—8 counts.
   d. Extend the arms and torso forward between the legs with a round back—8 counts.
   e. Curve and lean the torso over the right leg, bringing the right arm down and curved to the center of the body and extending the left arm overhead to stretch the side. Torso remains facing forward rather than facing down toward the right leg.
   f. Repeat e to the left.
   g. Combine d through f into a full circle stretch-swing, lean torso and arms to the right—count 1. Rotate torso and arms center—count 2 (*swinging motion*). Lean torso and arms to left—count 3. Lift torso and arms straight overhead—count 4.
   h. Repeat, reversing directions.

4 CTS.   4 CTS.

8. Sitting with legs crossed in a tailor-sit fashion. Have the right hand take hold of the inside of the right heel.
   a. Keeping the back straight, extend the right leg forward, keeping it turned out from the hip joint—4 counts.
   b. Return it to the original position—4 counts.
   c. Repeat a and b 4 times.
   d. Repeat a through c with the left heel and left hand.

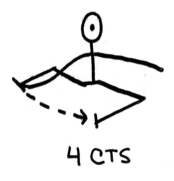

4 CTS

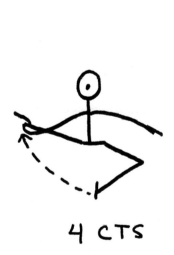

4 CTS

9. Sitting with legs crossed in a tailor-sit fashion. Have the right hand take hold of the inside of the right heel.
   a. Keeping the back straight, extend the right leg to the side of the body as far and as low to the ground as possible. Keep the leg turned out from the hip joint—4 counts.
   b. Return it to the original position—4 counts.
   c. Repeat a and b 4 times.
   d. Repeat a through c with the left heel and left hand.

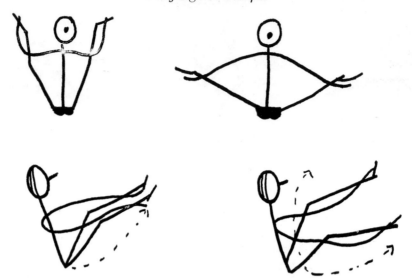

10. Sitting with the soles of the feet together, take hold of the inside heels with both hands (same hand, same heel). Keeping the back straight, extend both legs to the front of the body and in the air, emphasis on height. It is important that the muscles of the front and back of the body work in coordination and balance. If they are not holding in balance, the body will fall either forward or backward, depending which was not held strongly enough. Take 4 counts to extend upward and 4 counts to contract back to position.

11. Repeat number 10, extending the legs to a wide, low open position in the air. Take 4 counts to extend out and 4 counts to contract in. Note: Techniques 8 through 10 are for flexibility and strength.

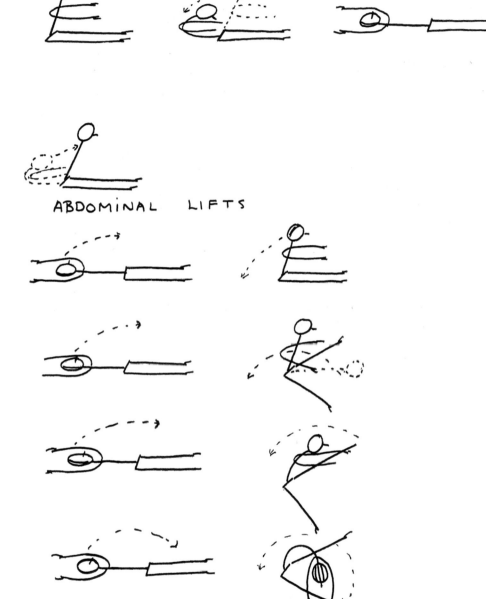

ABDOMINAL LIFTS

Strength

1. *Abdominal Lifts:* Sit, with legs extended on the floor in front. Round the spine (back) over the legs.
   a. Allow the spine to be lowered to the floor, one vertebra at a time, making sure that the lower back touches the floor and that the head remains forward until the last count.

b. Reverse the motion of "a" and round the back up from the floor to a position over the legs.

c. Alternate the counts used to do a and b. Begin with a set of 8 counts, 6 counts, 4 counts, 2 counts, 1 count, 1 count.

d. Repeat c with the legs in a bent position, feet on the floor.

e. Repeat the abdominal lifts with the legs alternating position as follows:

 —one set with the legs in a long, extended position.

 —one set with the legs in an extended position on the descent and opening to a wide open position on the lift.

 —one set with the legs in an extended position on the descent and opening on the lift with the torso reaching over the right leg.

 —one set with the legs in an extended position on the descent and opening on the lift with the torso reaching over the left leg.

 —Use two counts for each set (both the up and down motion), e.g., two counts down and two counts up

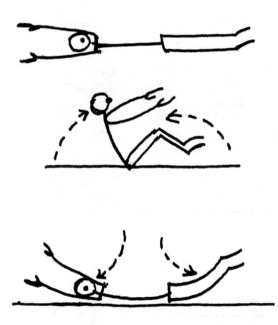

2. *The Arch:* Body is in a supine position (on the back) to start.

a. Contract the body in one motion to a position balanced on the coccyx (tailbone). Legs are in a bent-knee position off the ground and the arms are extended to the side of the knees; the back is straight—count 1.

b. Rotate the body to the right, opening it and extending it into an arched position, balanced on the right hip—count 2.

c. Return to the coccyx position (described in a)—count 3.

d. Extend the body to a supine position—count 4.

e. Repeat a through d (entire sequence) arching to the left side.

CT. 1-2-3   CT. 1   CT. 2-3

CT. 1   CT. 2-3   CT. 1   CT. 2-3   CT. 1

CT. 2-3   CT. 1   CT. 1-3

3. *Cross-over to a Stand* (development): Sitting position, back straight, knees bent and feet firmly on the floor, legs are parallel, arms extended to each side.

   a. Roll the right hip to the right side and cross the left leg over the right thigh, touching the left foot on the floor to the right side— count 1, 2, 3.

   b. Roll the left hip to the left side, bringing the left leg back to its original position and crossing the right leg over the left thigh, touching the right foot on the floor to the left side—counts 1, 2, 3.

   c. Repeat a and b several times.

   d. Extend the motion of a and b to raise the body onto the knee of each side. The motion is a rocking motion developing into a lift, then rocking to the other side and developing into a knee lift. 3 counts for each side.

   e. Extend the motion of d to raise the body through the knee position and into a stand. Then reversing the motion and standing to the other side. 3 counts for each side.

f. Take the 3 basic positions and combine them. Do two sets of each position.

It should be noted that all the swing combinations and much of the rhythm section can also be center floor activities and combinations. The techniques given here are suggestions of movement which have proven to be effective. It is hoped that each teacher will develop her own techniques and combinations or alter these to meet the needs of each individual class. Each teacher should strive to find her own style of teaching and suit the technique to the skills and age levels of her classes.

LOCOMOTOR PROGRESSIONS TECHNIQUE

Based on Developmental Patterns

The following are suggestions for progressions and developments of various basic developmental patterns. The combinations and variations are endless. Most of the ideas will come from your class. The most important role of the teacher is to focus the class on a problem or motivation and stimulate them to move to it in their own way. If the progressions are technical rather than creative, then proper technique should be demonstrated and learned. The technical skills then will carry through into the more expressive aspects of dance and allow each person to extend his range of movement possibilities. It is also important to emphasize that a person have a definite starting position and ending position in order to complete the idea of a beginning, middle and ending.

1. Think of the basic developmental patterns that progress *through* space, such as walking, running and skipping. Some different directions in which each can be done are:
   a. forward
   b. backward
   c. diagonally left and right
   d. up and down
   e. circularly

2. Combine any two basic steps together. Try several variations with your class.

3. Choose a motivation and build and combine basic patterns together to create a repetitious phrase of movement which progresses across the floor.

4. Change the floor pattern of the movement as it progresses.

5. Explore the rhythm of the patterns you and your class have developed. Clap the rhythm in a repetitious pattern.

6. Vary the way your class moves across the floor.
   a. on the diagonal.
   b. one person moving from each diagonal simultaneously—crossing, as in an X.
   c. two people moving from opposite diagonals; moving in opposite directions in toward each other.

d. people moving from the four corners of the room to the opposite corners.

e. partners moving across the floor.

f. lines of people moving towards each other.

g. groups of people moving together.

7. Change the tempo of the locomotor patterns.

8. Take the same movement or combination and vary the motivation (reason or feeling).

Walks and Turns

Beginning

1. Have each person walk across the floor in his own way, finishing in a bow or shape.

2. Do walks in various *directions*. First walk in one direction at a time, then combine two directions together (forward and backward).

3. Change the *tempo* of the walks (fast walks; slow walks).

4. Without a specific beat, allow each person to do his own tempo in walking, running, etc.

5. Have the class take *big* steps and *little* steps, first separately and then in combined ways (e.g., big, little, little) or (e.g., 4 slow counts of big walks and 8 fast counts for little walks—4 quarter notes and 8 eighth notes). Size like tempo is relative.

6. Add directional changes for the above (5).

7. Use *emotional motivations* for creating different types of walks, eg., angry walks; sad walks; in a hurry, etc. Be aware of the tempo and amount of force used for each. Try other kinds of movements to express each feeling, eg., *sad:* turns, falls or *angry:* kicks, jumps. Combine these with the walks.

Intermediate

1. Walk a combination of 4 walks forward and 4 walks backward. Progress in this pattern across the floor. When starting on right foot, turn right. Reverse for the left side.

a. Combination of 2 walks forward and 2 walks backward.

b. Combination of 1 walk forward and 1 walk backward. Make sure that person looks both front and back as progressing. This is a *turn*.

c. *Turn:* step forward on right foot—count 1.

spin on left foot to complete turn.

focus is now front only (spotting).

repeat, turn left, beginning with left foot.

2. Have each person choose two basic movements to put together into their own pattern, e.g., *walk* and *turn*.

3. Refer to Beginning Walks number 7. Have each person in the class choose an emotion and then combine two or three basic movements to

express that feeling, e.g., *happy:* skip, run and jump. Allow each person to put the movements together in any way he chooses, letting the feeling motivate him.

4. Walk across the floor in diagonals across an imaginary center line.
   a. Partners walk the same diagonal path together.
   b. Partners walk opposite diagonal paths together.
   c. Repeat b and have partners touch hands as they meet.
   d. Repeat a through c running (double time).

Advanced

1. Partners walk diagonally away and toward each other, 4 counts each direction.
   a. Vary the *tempo* in different ways, such as fast out and slow in.
   b. Run the pattern, rather than walking (double time).
   c. Have each partner be motivated by a specific emotion, such as fear. Alter the tempo accordingly.
   d. Have the partners cross each other's path and continue in an X pattern.
   e. Repeat the X pattern in d, using a change of body direction in space, eg., X pattern with the body facing backward or a combination of forward and backward.

2. Refer to Intermediate Walks number 3. Extend the combinations of movement into a more extended structure by expanding the various *elements*.

3. Have the group move across the floor in partners.
   a. Each partner chooses a feeling and relate to the other as they dance across the floor.
   b. One partner moves for 4 counts and hold for 4 counts while partner does the opposite. Each relates to the other with a specific motivation.

4. Turn to the right for 3 counts.
   Turn to the left for 3 counts.
   (Take three steps to complete each turn, ending front.)
   This is an extension of the *walking turn.*

5. *Hip-turn* (lead-up is at the barre): Step right forward, left leg lifting (hip under and leg bent back) and turning back. Left shoulder leads turn-back while right shoulder is angled downward and acts like a pivot. Turn is initiated at the hip as it turns over. The count is: step—count 1; hip-turn—count 2.
   a. Repeat above to each direction separately.
   b. Add the same arm as leg taking step in a circle over the head. (Circle goes counter-clockwise over head, whipping with the hip-turn).
   c. Dip the torso down low on the turn.

Runs

Beginning

1. Have each person run forward across the floor.
2. Have each person run backward across the floor.
3. Have each person run forward and change to backward halfway while continuing in same direction.
4. Have each person run to the half-way point, do a slow fall to the ground, rise, and run to the end of the space.
5. Have children run a large circle around the space of the room, continuing to run in circles of decreasing sizes until they are turning in a very small space.
6. Reverse number 5, having the children begin in a very small circle and make it increasingly larger. Emphasize that the smaller the space, the smaller the steps and the larger the space, the larger the steps.
7. Have the class think of reasons they might run, e.g., in fear or to explore, letting the motivation determine the way they run and also the way they use space and directions.
8. Have each person in class choose his own reason for running. Each person dance their own idea.
9. Try runs in which various elements of dance are changed or emphasized, e.g., run in slow motion; run with body leaning backward; run with body very low and small.

Intermediate

1. Have class divided into groups facing each other at opposite corners of the room. Two people from opposite corners run toward each other. As they cross in the center, turn and run backwards to the opposite corner.
2. Repeat the above with an *emotional motivation*.
3. Give a specific rhythm to the run, such as a 3/4 meter, letting the first beat be accented with a tilt of the body to the side. The tilt will be on opposite sides every three counts.
   Run right—count 1, tilt right.
   Run left—count 2.
   Run right—count 3.
   Run left—count 1, tilt left.
   Run right—count 2.
   Run left—count 3.
   Repeat diagonally across the floor, then in a circle.
4. Repeat number 3 in 6/8 time (faster tempo, accents on count 1 and count 4).
5. Repeat number 4, doing the first measure facing forward—3 counts and the second measure facing backward—3 counts.
   a. Count 1 and 2, run forward.

b. Turn to back on count 3 (one half turn moving toward the direction of foot stepped on in count 1).
c. Right-left-right (turn to the right) on counts 1, 2, 3.
d. Count 4 and 5, run backward.
e. Turn to front on count 6 (one half turn continuing to turn in the same direction, completing a full circle).

Advanced

1. Do the waltz run with a turn, leaping on count 1.
2. Facing front, run a spiral circular path using six counts to complete each part of the spiral. This may be walked in large steps first. A leap may be added on count 1. When moving the circle to the right, begin with the right foot, ending on count 6 with left foot and progressing across the floor.
3. Clap a specific rhythm, repeating it until it is "felt." Without counting the rhythm out, run it across the floor holding for the same amount of time. Repeat.
4. Combine runs with holds (stillness). Add the body leaning in different directions until balance is lost and then running in that direction instead of taking the loss of balance into a fall, e.g., run-stop-lean- and run. Allow different parts of the body to lead you off balance, e.g., hip.

Gallops and Slides

Beginning

1. Each person gallops across the floor, leading with same leg the entire way. Repeat with other leg leading.
2. Gallop 4 times on one leg and 4 times on the other, continuing pattern across the floor.
3. Gallop 2 times on each foot, turning the gallop into a two-step. If a hop is emphasized at the end of each gallop (hop-slide-slide) it then becomes a Polka step.
4. Do the gallop sideways to become a *slide*. This is difficult for small children.
5. Slide across the room with the right side leading. Repeat with the left side leading.
6. Alternate sides every 4 slides, still moving in the same direction.
7. Do number 6 with a partner, facing and away, but not holding hands.
8. Do number 7, changing sides every 2 counts, while continuing in the same direction.
9. Do number 8 with a partner, holding back hands. Slide facing partner and away from partner. Change sides with partner so that each moves facing the opposite direction.
10. Try number 7 through number 9 with several different partners, because each person moves in a different way.

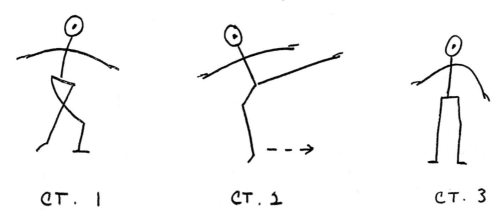

CT. 1   CT. 2   CT. 3

Intermediate

1. Variation on the basic slide: move sideways (side leading). If sliding to the right: (cross-slide-step)
   a. Cross left foot in front of right—count 1.
   b. Slide on the left foot—count 2.
   c. Step to the side with right foot—count 3.
   d. Reverse the above when moving to the left.
2. Repeat 1, adding the arms crossing in front of the body as the leg crosses over. Arms open to the side and stay open for the slide and step. (cross, open, open) The emphasis on this slide is *low* and *long* with the body.

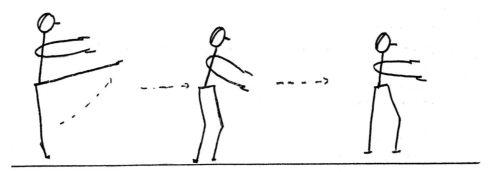

3. *One-legged skip* (variation on the gallop and slide) facing forward.
   a. Facing front, step forward with the right foot—count 1.
   b. Slide forward on the right foot while lifting the left leg straight into the air—count 1-and.
   c. Step left foot front—count 2.
   d. Continue on the same side, progressing forward with the *emphasis on height*. The slide actually becomes a large hop (slide-hop-step).

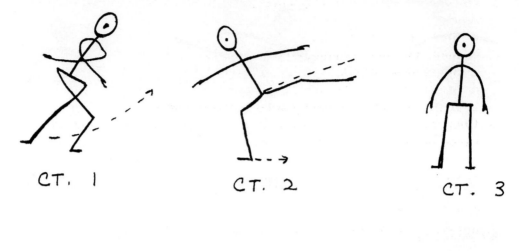

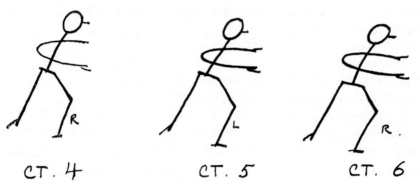

Advanced

1. *Cross-slide-step combination alternating sides* (see slides for Intermediate Progressions 1).
   a. Cross right foot over left—count 1 (left side is leading).
      Slide right (high hop)—count 2-and.
      Step left—count 3.
   b. Face direction you are moving in and
      Run right—count 4
      Run left—count 5.
      Run right—count 6.
   c. Cross left foot over right—count 1 (right side is leading).
      Slide left (high hop)—count 2-and.
      Step right—count 3.
   d. Face direction you are moving in and
      Run right—count 4.
      Run left —count 5
      Run right—count 6.
      Repeat sequence across the floor.

2. *One-legged skip, alternating sides* (refer to Slides Intermediate Progressions 3).
   a. Step right—count 1.
   b. Slide-hop right—count 1-and.
   c. Step left—count 2.
   d. Step right—count 2-and.
   e. Repeat on left, alternating sides across the floor.
3. Combine the *cross-slide-step* with the *one legged skip* (alternate between facing side and facing front).

Jumps

Beginning

Jumps should be learned at barre or in place, as with skips.
1. Jump across the room facing forward.
2. Jump across the room facing backward, but progressing forward.
3. Use other directional changes with jumps, such as side to side or circular.
4. Briefly talk about: animals that jump; bugs that jump; objects or machines with a jump-like quality or motion; emotional motivation that would stimulate jumping; feelings that would make you jump. Take one of the above ideas and have the members of the class jump across the floor with a motivation.

Intermediate

1. Do jumps across the floor, 4 forward (facing front) and 4 backward, progressing in the same direction.
   a. Repeat, doing 2 jumps in each direction.
   b. Repeat, doing 1 jump in each direction, continuing the turn in a full circle, while progressing forward.
2. Have each person create a *jump pattern* (a series of jumps that is repeated the same way and with the same rhythm), e.g., jump apart-together-together-turn in air; jump apart-together-together-turn in air (turning jump), etc.

Advanced

1. Do the spread-jump combination (center floor development) across the floor: combination of 3 straight jumps and one wide leg spread jump in air (position in the air is sitting, legs open, arms reaching for toes).
2. Jump into the air through space, arching the body as the jump is performed.
3. Have the class develop a specific jump-combination using leaps, runs, hops, skips, turns in a specific pattern. Have the entire class follow and learn each of the combinations.

Hops and Skips

Beginning

Preparation for hops and skipping should be done at barre or in place.

1. Hops are a prerequisite to learning to skip. Each person should hop across the room on each foot separately.
2. Do hops on alternating feet, lifting each knee high in turn (1–2, 1–2). This should be done first at barre or in place, then in progression. When the step-hop is speeded up it becomes a skip and the rhythm becomes uneven rather than even.
3. When the skip is learned, do the following:
   a. Skip across the floor forward.
   b. Skip backward.
   c. Skip turning to the right (review the walking turn first).
   d. Skip turning to the left.
   e. Combine 4 skips forward with 4 turning skips.
4. Teach a simple skipping combination to group in circle or to be done with partners, e.g., *circle formation.*
   a. Skip into the center of circle—4 counts.
   b. Skip back out—4 counts.
   c. Repeat.
   d. Each person skips a circle around themselves to right—4 counts.
   e. Each person skips a circle around themselves to left—4 counts.
   f. Repeat combination.
   g. If done with partners, children can lock right and left elbows on the skips in a circle.
5. Have each person skip a large circular pattern around the room, either alone or with a small group.
   a. Skip inside a circle formed by the rest of the class.
   b. Skip outside a circle formed by the rest of the class.
   c. Add arm movements which either trace a circular motion in space or swing across the body in an open-closed motion.
   d. Have the class explore other ways to coordinate the arms with a skip.
   e. Vary the floor pattern.

Intermediate

1. Teach the *skip-turn* with an emphasis on timing and position of the body. First do in 3/4 meter, then in 6/8 meter.
   a. Step right (turns will be to the right)—count 1.
   b. Hop right, turning one-half turn to right—count 2, 3 (now facing back).
   c. Step left—count 1 (foot reaches behind body toward direction of progression.
   d. Hop left, turning one-half turn to right to complete full circle—count 2, 3.

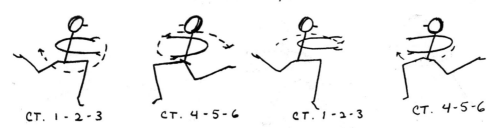

CT. 1 - 2 - 3   CT. 4 - 5 - 6   CT. 1 - 2 - 3   CT. 4 - 5 - 6

2. Combine the waltz run with the skip-turn in 6/8 meter.
   a. Run right—count 1 (accent).
   b. Run left—count 2.
   c. Run right—count 3.
   d. Run left—count 4 (accent).
   e. Run right—count 5.
   f. Run left—count 6.
   g. Step right—count 1.
   h. Hop right (one-half turn to right)—count 2 and 3.
   i. Step left—count 4.
   j. Hop left (one-half turn, completing turn to front)—count 5 and 6.
   k. Repeat entire sequence.

Leaps

Beginning

Lead-up for leaps can be given at barre.
1. Have the class run with long steps, turning the run into leaps.
2. Place a real or imaginary barrier in the center of the room on the floor. Have the members of the class run and leap to get over the barrier. Stress the action of taking off on one foot and landing on the other, as in a large run or a slow-motion run. When this concept is understood, speed up the leap and stress length rather than height as at first.
3. Try low, long leaps.
4. Try high leaps.
5. Let the class combine runs and leaps in their own pattern.

Intermediate

1. Have the class clap and say the rhythmic pattern of *short-short-long*, (rhythmic pattern can be *1 and 2*). Take the pattern into movement across the floor, using a *walk*. This would consist of two short walks and one long walk.
2. When 1 is accomplished in a walk, have the class *run* the pattern, taking the *long* into the air (reaching forward in space rather than up). Run-run-leap.

3. Do the waltz run in 6/8 meter, leaping on counts 1 and 4. Add two one-half turns.

Advanced

1. Combine the *leap* with a *spin-turn*.
   a. Leap on count 1 (forward).
   b. Spin-turn on count 2 (full circle turn toward the direction of leg leap was taken on).
   c. Continue the above across the floor, taking each direction separately.

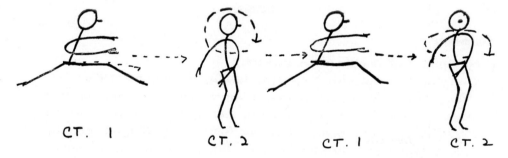

2. Combine *leap-spin-turn* with *2 sets of waltz runs* in 6/8 meter.
   a. Begin on right foot.
   b. Run forward—counts *1, 2, 3*.
   c. Run forward—counts *4, 5, 6*.
   d. Leap right—count 1.
   e. Spin-turn (to right)—count 2, 3.
   f. Leap right—count 4.
   g. Spin-turn (to right)—count 5, 6.
   h. Repeat on left side.

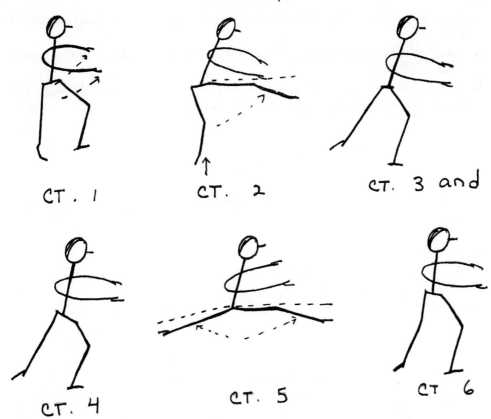

CT. 1 CT. 2 CT. 3 and

CT. 4 CT. 5 CT 6

3. Combine the *one-legged skip* with the *leap*.
   a. Step right—count 1.
   b. Hop right—count 2.
   c. Step left—count 3 and.
   d. Step right—count 4.
   e. Leap left—count 5.
   f. Land on left foot—count 6.
   g. Continue pattern across floor. Repeat on other side.

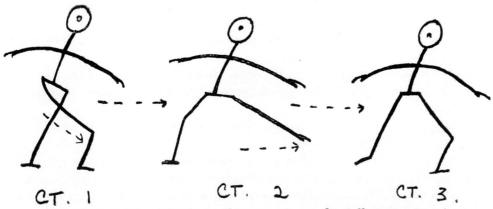

CT. 1 CT. 2 CT. 3.

(See instructions for these three steps on the following page.)

4. Repeat 3, alternating sides. Add an extra step after the leap—count 6 and.
5. Leap side to side, moving leaps diagonally forward as you progress across the floor.
6. Repeat the cross-slide-step, substituting the leap for the slide. This becomes *cross-leap; cross-leap.* Alternate sides.

7. *Arch* the back while the body is in the air during the leap. Emphasis in this leap is on height as well as length.

RHYTHM

Think of rhythm. It is different for every person. Think of tempo. It is different for every person (relative). How fast can a movement be done? How slowly? Both of these extremes are relative to each person.
1. Move a combination of fast and slow movements.
2. Move and hold still for equal number of counts.
3. Move and hold still for unequal numbers of counts or period of time.
4. Clap or create a rhythm and repeat it.
5. Put the same rhythm into your arms and other body parts. Into your feet. Into your feet and torso.
6. Move in a particular rhythm through space. Change directions. Do this with a partner. Do this in opposition to a group or a partner. Do this in a round.
7. Change the tempo of a rhythm. Slow it down and speed it up or progressively change the tempo.
8. Start with a feeling and allow the feeling to create a rhythm or a tempo.
The following are suggestions for teaching rhythm. Each group, no matter what the ability, can achieve satisfaction and challenge from creating rhythms and discovering new ones from others. Movement may grow out

of a rhythm or the movement itself may create rhythm. Feelings and ideas motivate different tempos and rhythmic patterns.

Rhythm

Beginning

1. Sit in a circle. Have each person say his first name. Clap or beat beaters or drums in the basic rhythm of each name with the whole group participating.
2. Ask the class to hear the *number of sounds* in each name.
3. When all the names are known, clap and say each name a specific number of times (e.g., 3 times). Go around the circle saying each name 3 times without stopping in between names: succession of changing rhythms is the result.
4. After several sessions of clapping first names, progress to the rhythmic pattern of *first and last names.*
5. Using hands, beaters or drums do the following:
    a. Beat a very fast tempo.
    b. Beat a very slow tempo.
    c. Beat a very slow tempo and get progressively faster until the class is beating as fast as possible. Reverse the progression.
    d. Beat a very loud beat.
    e. Beat a very soft beat.
    f. Combine the voice with d and e. Start soft and get louder with both voice and beat. Reverse.
    g. Combine loud and soft beats into a rhythmic pattern such as *loud, soft, soft*. Repeat several times.
    h. Count a specific number of counts. Ask the class to make the first beat loud (accent) and the other beat soft, e.g., 5 counts would be loud, soft, soft, soft, soft. Repeat the pattern.
    i. Take a specific number of counts and have the class beat only the first beat each time (accent).
    j. Beat a specific number of counts and hold or be silent for the same number of counts, e.g., clap for 4 counts and hold for 4 counts.
6. Develop each of the above in number 5 into movement using various body parts: feet; whole body; moving through space. In number 5, it should be emphasized to *hold* the body in a definite position or shape.
7. In a circle, have each person clap a specific number of counts alone. Have the class clap in succesion without stopping the pattern.
8. Take the same count as in number 7 and clap one measure on the beat and one measure any way you want within the 4 counts.
9. In a circle, have each person walk or skip into the center, first as a group, then individually in succession.
10. Repeat number 9 with *variations:*
    a. Change the tempo from slow to fast.

b. Let each person move in and out of the circle, using the same number of counts but doing any movement he wants.

c. Each person moves in and out with a specific emotion as the motivation is suggested, e.g., feeling angry or feeling silly.

d. Entire group moves into the center very slowly and out very quickly, ending in various shapes. A particular emotion may be added, such as *fear*. Reverse the progression and move in quickly and out slowly.

e. One person at a time dances into the center and hold their position or shape until each person is in the circle, then all dance out together or individually. Use a specific count.

11. In a circle, each person may have a chance to dance alone in the center, choosing to dance to either a fast or slow tempo. You may have the class all dance to a slow tempo first and then dance to a fast tempo.

12. In a circle, each person may have a specific number of counts or measures to move to a particular accompaniment or to any rhythm he creates for himself as he dances.

13. Each person may choose two basic movements and combine them in his own way into a pattern, e.g., *skip and turn*. These could be done separately by skipping for 4 counts and turning for 4 counts or they could be combined into a skipping turn. Each person will combine them in his own way and form a unique pattern.

14. Repeat number 13 and add a feeling to the two movements. The movements and feelings must be related. For example, if someone chooses to feel sad, he should not pick jumps or hops.

15. Use various instruments and sounds and discover the difference in quality of each, even though they might play the same rhythm. Explore and develop the qualities into extended movements. First capture the *quality* of each different sound, then add specific rhythms, e.g., a gong has a percussive (accent) beginning sound and extends into a sustained quality. Once this is explored, then the gong can be hit in a specific rhythm and this also can be put into dance.

16. Take a particular movement and do it for a specific number of counts, e.g., turn to the right for 4 counts; turn to the left for 4 counts.

17. Take a particular movement and vary the counts in a changing pattern.

a. Jump 8 counts. Hold for 8 counts.

b. Jump 6 counts. Hold for 6 counts.

c. Jump 4 counts. Hold for 4 counts.

d. Jump 2 counts. Hold for 2 counts.

e. Jump 1 count. Hold for 1 count.

f. Jump 1 count. Hold for 1 count.

g. Repeat the series. Add directional changes.

18. Take several basic movements and combine them into a short phrase that is within the range of your class, e.g., total group in a circle or groups of 4 or in partners.

PHRASE:

a. Skip into the circle 4 counts (forward).

b. Skip out of the circle 4 counts (backward).

c. Repeat.

d. Slide 8 counts to the right.

e. Slide 8 counts to the left.

f. Turn in place by yourself 8 counts to the right.

g. Turn in place by yourself 8 counts to the left.

h. Finish the 8th count by holding a definite body shape.

i. Vary the above by changing the tempo; substituting skips for walks; have each person dance in the center after the turns while the others clap; add another movement to the phrase to develop it further.

19. Do the basic locomotor skills and have the class determine the rhythm of each. Discover which are even rhythms and which are uneven. Have several students perform the movements while the others clap the rhythm.

Intermediate

1. Use hands, beaters or drums. Have each person create his own rhythm (repetition of a pattern of beats). Have the entire group join in the rhythm, repeating several times.

2. Have one person, several people or the entire group put the individual rhythms into a body part; into the feet while sitting or standing. Have them move the rhythm through space or around the circle. Feet must move *only* on the beats in the rhythm. Dance the rhythm with the entire body. Then add a *feeling* to the rhythm.

3. Change the tempo of each rhythm. Add direction changes. Change the feeling. The movements will be changed by these factors even though the rhythm remains the same.

4. Take 8 counts and develop a specific combination using half time, quarter time, double time, and accent, e.g., 8 counts or 2 measures of 4.

a. 2 measures—walk on the *accent* only.

b. 2 measures—walk on *every other beat* (half time).

c. 2 measures—walk on *every beat* (quarter time).

d. 2 measures—walk on *two beats to every count* (double time).

e. Combine these—a through d into a phrase and repeat.

5. Repeat number 4 with the following *variations:*

a. Double each part of the above phrase, doing each part forward and then backward.

b. Add a reason or feeling to the combination, e.g., the feeling of *anger:* it would be moved differently during the slow part of the phrase than during the fast conclusion of the phrase.

c. Vary the space, directions or floor pattern, e.g., change direction every two measures.

  d. Do the combination with another person, each doing his own
     movements, but to the same rhythm while relating to each other.
  e. Each person decides upon a specific emotion *before* relating to a
     partner, then relate to partner expressing that emotion.
6. Refer to *Move and Hold Pattern* (Beginning Progressions—number 5).
   Extend that pattern in the following ways:
  a. Have the entire group move and hold together, as relating in move-
     ment and in shape (like statues).
  b. Alter the tempo from slow to fast.
  c. Divide the group in half. Group I moves while Group II holds and
     vice versa (like a Rondo Form—round).
  d. Decide upon a particular tempo and rhythm or feeling for the moti-
     vation.
  e. Organize the group into partners, with one moving for a specific
     number of counts while the other holds the same number of counts.
     Partners relate with specific feeling or tempo given. Space may be
     used in any way. Use directions and levels and shape as well as
     rhythm and feeling.
  f. In partners, have one person move (other holding) to 8 slow beats;
     partner responds (while first partner holds position) by moving for
     16 fast beats. The number of counts chosen can vary. Have each
     person have a chance to experience both the fast and slow part of
     the combination.
7. Beat a specific rhythm on the drum and have the class move to that
   rhythm. Try out several different rhythms and tempos.
8. Use a record or accompaniment to give several different types of qualities, tempos and rhythms. Have the class move to each and change
   from one to another.
9. See Beginning Progressions number 9. Develop the same idea in the
   following ways:
  a. Increase the number of measures from 2 to 4.
  b. Encourage each person to use the space within the circle and out-
     side the circle in any way he wants.
  c. Have each person relate to the others in the circle as he dances.
  d. Have each person in the circle begin two measures apart rather than
     four measures. This means that two will be moving at one time for
     part of their sequence.
  e. Let each person end up anywhere he wants to, holding in a par-
     ticular shape or position.
  f. Give each person only 4 counts and have him move into the center
     of the circle and end in a shape at any level he chooses. Each per-
     son, in succession, then relates to the first person without touching.
     The entire group is ending in a group shape or design.
  g. Repeat f, adding a specific emotion and tempo for the entire group
     to choreograph. When all are in the center design, they again take

turns dancing out and into a finished shape or position. Entire group can move out of the design together or it can be decided by spontaneously taking turns and relating in movement to each other as they progress.

    h. The above idea can be extended to smaller groups within the class. For example, the class may be divided into groups of 4 or 6 people. A different starting position, other than a circle may also be determined. The counts may be varied and the entrances and exits may be changed.

10. Any rhythm may be chosen or created and done in the following ways:
    a. Unison.
    b. Echo sequence (original rhythm followed by same rhythm in answer).
    c. Rondo form (a round).
    d. Opposing rhythms.

11. Take 4 measures of a specific number of counts. Assign a particular basic movement to each measure, e.g.,
    a. measure 1—turn.
    b. measure 2—fall.
    c. measure 3—rise.
    d. measure 4—hold.
    e. repeat the sequence.

12. Take the same form and sequence of number 11. Add tempo changes and a specific feeling. The quality and the tempo and rhythm of the movement will be changed because of the different motivations, e.g.,
    a. Feeling of silliness—fast tempo, irregular rhythm.
    b. Feeling of sadness—slow tempo, fairly even rhythm.
    c. Feeling of happiness—medium tempo, even rhythm.
Allow the class to decide what tempo changes they want for each feeling.

13. Explore the relationship of rhythm, space, tempo and feelings. Allow the feelings to create and determine the tempo and rhythm as well as the movements themselves.

14. Let different members of the class create a movement which has a repetitive rhythmic pattern. All clap and accompany the movement, allowing the movement to determine any changes.

Advanced

1. Teach specific meters, such as 2/4, 3/4, 4/4, 5/4 and 6/8. Put each of these into a phrase of music. Create movement and rhythm within the specific meter being used. Learn the movement so that it can be repeated exactly the same way. Add another phrase onto the first, developing the movement into a short dance. Each person in class can develop the original phrase by choreographing another section from the ending point of the last movement. This is an exercise in group

choreography. Each person learns the original movement and takes turns adding onto it. It can then be repeated from start to finish, with entrances, directional space changes, tempo changes and quality changes being used to vary and extend the group choreography.

2. Alternate two different meters such as: 4/4, 3/4. Repeat.
3. Oppose two different meters. Divide the group into two or more groups. One group moves for 4 measures of 3/4 (3 counts); the other group moves for 3 measures of 4/4 (4 counts), equalling 12 counts for each group.
   a. Have the two groups move on every beat of their section.
   b. Have the two groups move only on the accents of their section.
   c. Have the two groups create their own rhythms within their section.
4. Take two measures of 6/8 meter and divide each measure up in a different way, e.g.,
   a. measure 1—count and accent every 3 counts.
   b. measure 2—count and accent every 2 counts.
   c. result: 1—2—3—4—5—6
   　　　　　　 1—2—3—4—5—6
5. Repeat number 4 with the following variations:
   a. Walk or run the above pattern. Use directional changes.
   b. Combination of *steps* and *hops*.

   Step R, Hop R, Step L
   　1　　　2　　　3

   Step R, Hop R, Step L
   　4　　　5　　　6

   Step R, Hop R
   　1　　　2

   Step L, Hop L
   　3　　　4

   Step R, Hop R
   　5　　　6

   Repeat the pattern from the beginning with the left foot. Continue across the floor, alternating the pattern from the right to the left.
   c. Repeat number 2 with direction changes or feelings added.
   d. Pattern of the *Waltz Run* and *Step-Hop Turns:* See Intermediate Locomotor Progressions, Skipping section number 2.
   e. Do the same rhythmic pattern with leaps.

   Leap R, Run L, Run R
   　1　　　2　　　3

   Leap L, Run R, Run L
   　4　　　5　　　6

   Leap R, Leap L, Leap R
   　1–2　　3–4　　5–6

   f. Do *Leap-spin-turn* with *2 sets of waltz runs.* Refer to Advanced Locomotor Progressions, Leaping section number 2.

g. *Two 6/8 runs forward* combined with *three cross-leaps* to the side.

Run R, Run L, Run R
  1   2   3

Run L, Run R, Run L
  4   5   6

Cross R foot over L to side. Leap to side with L
  1   2

Repeat 3–4

Repeat 5–6

Repeat the entire sequence several times, then repeat beginning L.

6. Refer to the *Move and Hold Pattern* (Intermediate 5). Develop this pattern by having the partners progress across the floor, using space in whatever way they wish.

   a. A specific tempo may be set for each one to move to.
   b. Select a particular feeling for the entire group. Use the feeling as the motivation.
   c. Each couple can move and relate spontaneously to each other, exaggerating their movements into dance.
   d. Each couple may choose the same emotion or opposing emotions to use as the motivation.

7. Refer to Intermediate number 9f through number 9h. Develop by giving each person a limited time to move out into space from the corner of the room. Use a feeling quality or tempo as motivation. Each person moves individually, relating to the others in the group and attaching onto their design (touch may or may not be used). The entire group may begin from the same corner or from other parts of the room. Each person may leave the group separately or on a specific count or finish in the design itself, e.g., if the emotion of *fear* were chosen, the first person would dance out from the corner, motivated by the feeling of fear, finishing in a related shape or position.

   The second person then dances out from the corner. He might *react* in fear to the person already out on the floor, or be motivated by the same type of fear as the other. He may be repelled by the first (this will be seen in the movement) or seek him out as security for comfort from his own fear.

   The ideas will be as varied and as individual as the people in the class. If the emotion is motivating them, the ideas will clearly be seen through movement. If they are unsure of their own motivation, this will result in movement which appears ambivalent.

8. Create or find a record or have the accompanist play a rhythmic piece that has an ABA or ABC or ABAC form. Create a dance in which the A sections are alike in either quality or exact choreography and the B section is different in quality and movements. After exploring the idea of *contrast,* choreograph a dance with one of these forms as the structure.

9. Take two contrasting feelings and put them into a dance, using a *pro-*

gression from one feeling to another, or an *abrupt change* or an *alternation.*

10. Take a particular number of counts and discover through dance all the possible rhythmic variations and combinations within the number of counts, e.g., 5 counts:

> 1 count and 4 counts
> 2 counts and 3 counts
> 3 counts and 2 counts
> 4 counts and 1 count
> 5 counts moving
> 5 counts holding still

You can place the *accents on various counts,* putting this into accented movement.

a. The accent could progress to a different count every measure of 5.

<u>1</u> 2 3 4 5 1 <u>2</u> 3 4 5 1 2 <u>3</u> 4 5 1 2 3 <u>4</u> 5

b. Let each person create a rhythm to the 5 counts. Create a phrase by combining several of these rhythms together.

FURTHER SOURCES FOR CREATIVE STIMULATION

1. Changes of direction: high-low-forward-backward-sideways.
2. Changes of shapes and floor patterns: circle-round; semi-circle-curve; triangle; square; straight line, zig-zag, diagonal; symmetrical-asymmetrical.
3. Changes in levels: high-low; up-down; medium-center; below-center; sit-squat-floor fall.
4. Changes in tempo (rate of speed): fast-medium-slow.
5. Changes in quality of movement (force): light-heavy-smooth-staccato-jerky-flowing-push-pull-swing-vibratory-sharp-strong-weak.
6. Changes in relationship: alone-solo-partners-small groups-large groups.
7. Combinations of movement: walk-run; run-run-leap; step-hop; jump-hop; skip-turn, etc.
8. Object or thought motivations: leaves-floating-flowing, wood, stones, sea-shells, clouds, sand, grass, wind, rain, sun, hills, waves-water.
9. Sound: percussion instruments, gongs-drums-cymbals-woodblocks-whistles-bells-triangles-tambourines, etc.
10. Exploring color: relating color, thoughts and feelings.
11. Textures: sandpaper-burlap-velvet-silk-yarn, etc.
12. Stories: written and original. Poems: written and original.
13. Music or rhythmic patterns: composed or original.
14. Seasonal holidays: Valentines-St. Patrick's-Easter-July 4th-Halloween-Thanksgiving-Christmas, etc. Seasons: Winter-Spring-Summer-Fall.
15. Imitation of various objects, characters, animals, people: toys-clowns-witches-puppets-dogs-snakes-elephants-balls-balloons-feathers-old people-young people, etc.
16. Combinations of any or all of these various motivations for creative thinking and moving.

SAMPLE CLASSES

Two and Three Year Olds—Sample Class

Begin each class in a circle and introduce rhythm using drums or clapping (soft-loud, slow-fast, individual rhythms, and learning to follow other rhythms). Combine qualities and tempos, such as loud, soft, soft (3/4) or begin very slowly and progress to very fast, or lift sticks up and beat down. Say names in rhythm and beat or clap them out.

Warm-Ups

1. Touch and move isolated parts of the body. Vary the rhythm and tempo.
2. Use of direction awareness, such as up-down, circle around, side-side, forward-backward.
3. Shaking is a good warm-up movement—individual body parts.

Technique

1. Abdominal lifts.
2. Begin to introduce the side arch and the rocking arch on the stomach.
3. Teach rolls, change direction.
4. Creeping and crawling—front and back crawls.
5. Stretches—use different directions, such as upward, side, etc., reaching arms up, stretching over legs while sitting—closed and open.
6. Use the round shape and circle patterns (e.g., circle body parts or turn in a circle; sit in a circle; hold hands and walk or run together in a circle, turning, etc.
7. Rock—side to side in a sitting, standing, and moving situation. After rock is learned, change and vary tempo and rhythm and size. Front and back rock in sitting, standing positions, holding hands in circle and alone.
8. Teach jumps and introduce hops at barre (coordination and strength). Do jumps and hops without barre, progression. Vary.

Progressions

1. Introduce the diagonal line for progressions.
2. Walks—present self. Bow-curtsey. Variations in walking, such as backward and with partners.
3. Runs—use direction changes and combinations (circular, zig-zag, straight, front, back, side).
4. Gallops—right leg in front and change to left leg in front—direction changes.
5. Turns—basic turn, arms out.
6. Begin to combine large and small muscle work—coordinate, such as walking and moving arms or head.

7. Deal with size and quality of steps—big-little, heavy-light, fast-slow, and develop. Move and stop (hold), run and lift, run and squat.
8. Elementary partner work—walk with and toward and away from.

Creative Work

1. Story work—put qualities and ideas into movements and combine various movements to tell story through dance. Use of animals (e.g., elephants-heavy and slow; birds-light; giraffe-long neck-very tall; cats-creep-stretch-roll over-playful, etc.). Encourage and utilize children's ideas and develop such ideas as a trip to the beach, zoo, swimming, picnic, etc., as well as any other creative thoughts the children might have and want to express in dance. Keep ideas simple and short. Use feelings to stimulate movement.
2. Deal with size, shape, color, weight, words, space.

Instruments and Props

1. Use drums, shakers, clapping.
2. Use scarves, balloons, ribbons and other props to stimulate movement and teach colors. Beware of the danger of certain props—analyze before using (i.e., sharp items, strong rope, plastic).
3. Teach curtsey and bow.

Class Dance (simplified turn-around)

1. Hold partners' hands, run around in circle to the right—8 counts and then to the left—8 counts.
2. Partners hold both hands and gallop or slide—8 counts one direction and —8 counts other direction.
3. Turn by self—8 counts.
4. Bow or curtsey to partner—8 counts.

Four and Five Year Olds—Sample Class

Begin each class at barre. Start with awareness of body alignment (hips under, shoulders down, heads high, toes turned out).

Warm-Ups

1. Points with the foot (front, side, back) to work on coordination and direction. Let these develop into leg swings forward and back.
2. Separate and teach the head, arm swing combination. Teach each part separately—head swing in and out; add the arm swing in and out; outside arm reaching up; over; up and out.
3. Pliés—petit and grand, without arm movement (students can face the barre and perform with both hands holding).
4. Flat back stretches (hamstrings) facing the barre.
5. Develop the flat back position into a back leg lift.
6. Do side leg lift at barre.
7. Teach and develop knee bounces and heel bounces into jumps. Vary

the tempo and the rhythm, e.g., jump—2, hold—2 and other combinations.

8. Teach the hop on each leg. Develop into step-hop and then into the skip. Vary tempo and rhythm.

9. Introduce falls—first the side fall developed from reaching-over position. Emphasize placement of weight. Teach back fall if class is advanced.

10. Use skills such as jumps, hops, runs, skips or follow musical changes or a combination of quality and skills to move the class to a center-floor position (can be individual or group movement or follow the leader.)

Center Floor

Do center floor work in a circle (security and equality).

1. Touch and move isolated body parts. Either the teacher or individual students can initiate the movement within a given structure of rhythm or number of parts.

2. Structured stretches put into a rhythmic pattern, such as 8 bounces over straight legs; 8 over center in open leg position; 8 over each leg. Stretches should include hips, arms, back, legs and torso and combinations of these.

3. Abdominal lifts. Vary tempo and rhythm.

4. Introduce the coccyx lift (open and close).

5. Teach and review the side arch (lying on the floor) (open and close).

6. Introduce *falls* and *lifts* in various tempos and qualities.

7. Teach some standing balance, such as leg up—2 counts and down—2 counts. Develop the side rock and front-back rock so they extend to off-balance positions. Structure the number of counts for each balance problem.

8. Lift one leg to the back as a further development of the same movement at barre.

9. Begin to introduce swings, both side-and-side and frontback.

Rhythm

Use drums and other available instruments.

1. Work with individual rhythms, following and taking turns and learning basic rhythmic structure, such as 3/4 and 4/4. Develop into beating and holding rhythms. Do the same in movement (possibly body parts and walks).

2. Utilize measure structure for movement changes. Keep simple.

3. Utilize accent, tempo (fast-slow), some quality such as light-soft, heavy-strong, and some emotional relations to rhythm initiated by class, teacher, or pianist.

4. Utilize movement to get to corner for progressions.

Progressions

1. Walking—presenting self. Utilize variations of feelings to present self in different ways (silly, sad, happy, afraid, angry, shy, etc.).
2. Runs—use direction changes.
3. Walking with partners as well as in opposition to partner.
4. Gallop—alternating feet (2 step). Alone and with a partner.
5. Skips—begin to teach the skip moving backward. Combine the forward and backward skip. Add arm movements to the skip (coordination).
6. Turns—teach basic turn; then begin to work with basic concept of levels (high turn—on toes, very low turn); vary tempo—teach slow turn, such as step forward—2 steps and backward—2 steps.
7. Combine skips and turns.
8. Improvise ideas of movement combinations and tempos as well as learning teacher-directed combinations, e.g., combine any two movements together.
9. Work on falls, such as walk, stop and fall or turn and fall. Structure number of counts or structure as to tempo or quality.

Creative Work

1. Try to develop ideas growing out of the movement combinations as well moving to interpret ideas.
2. Use of stimuli, such as music, props, colors, sounds, and space limitations.

Class Dance "Turn Around"

1. Partners hook right arms (hands or elbows) and skip around to the right for 8 counts; then skip around to the left—8 counts.
2. Partners hold both hands and slide around to the right—8 counts; then slide to the left—8 counts.
3. Everyone turn in circle by self to the right—8 counts; then turn to the left—8 counts.
4. Use variations of movements and counts in combinations.
5. End with a bow or curtsey to partner.

Six and Eight Year Olds—Sample Class

Begin each class at barre.

Warm-Ups

1. Teach all the previous material with added development.
2. Teach the side leg swing (in and out).
3. Introduce leg and arm circles (forward and back circles), eg., front circle, back circle, front circle. Hold. Do separately and then together.
4. Vary the tempo and rhythm, as well as number of counts for the side and back fall.

5. Teach the brush-leap at barre; then have it move while using barre for support, eg., brush, leap, step.
6. Teach the lift and position of thigh (turned out) to the front and back on the step-hop (step-hop front and step-hop back) while facing the barre. Bounce knees first, develop into a bouncing rock; then into the step-hop.
7. Begin to develop the back leg lift into the roll turn (hip turn).

Center Floor

Do either in a circle or scattered spatial arrangement, facing front.
1. Introduce the head-arms-body swing combination. Head-swing right, swing left, swing all the way around; swing left, swing right, swing all the way around; add the arms with same sequence; add the whole body, and on the last swing, go into side fall to the ground (3/4 meter).
2. Combine some stretches together in sets. Vary the tempo and rhythm as well as the range.
3. Combine movements together within a set rhythmic structure:
   a. Turn
   b. Fall
   c. Rise or lift
   d. Skip or any type of locomotor movement.
   e. Use any variations and change the meter.
4. Combine the coccyx sit and the side arch together. From a lying position:
   a. Sit to coccyx—2 counts.
   b. Arch to right side—2 counts.
   c. Sit to coccyx—2 counts.
   d. Return to lying position—2 counts.
   e. Repeat to left.

Rhythm

1. Introduce other instruments and develop percussion into measure structure (use of accent). Do such things as having each person or group play or clap a set number of measures, then go onto the next group or individual without stopping, or have them clap or play so many together and so many individually, etc. Vary the meter and the tempo.
2. Have the class react to quality of sounds through movement.
3. Develop the rhythmic patterns into movement patterns:
   a. Move—3 counts.
   b. Hold—3 counts.
   c. Move only on the accent.
   d. Make a strong movement on the accent and smaller or lighter movements on the other counts.
   e. Move in double or half time, etc.

Progressions

1. Do all the previous progressions with more combinations. Structure creative work, such as doing any type of turn each desires but also have them decide the tempo and rhythm.
2. Use space to a greater degree—levels, range, patterns, crossing lines, shapes.
3. Introduce leaps and develop from barre exercise.

Creative Work

1. Add the idea of reason for their movement combinations and give it a rhythmic structure.
2. Begin to have the class work out stories on their own in groups, with various characters or roles.
3. Have class research a subject, i.e., the history of dance.
4. Have students explore different ways of dancing and let them choose their favorite style to dance.
5. Have the older students develop this into a studio performance.
6. The class dance for this age can have variations of combinations, movements and skills.

Psychiatric Patients—Sample Class

From the film script for
Body Ego Technique
Salkin-Salkin-Schoop

A typical class starts in a circle formation. This gives the patient a feeling of security.

Music helps to pull the group into a unit. It also stimulates unconscious qualities of movement. It releases tension, and it helps to guide the patients in their technique.

Beaters are used for rhythm. Individual rhythm is encouraged, as well as group participation.

Some of the patients hit the floor with all their strength. The opportunity to hit with the beaters seems to be a safe way for a patient to show his hostility.

The withdrawn patients hardly touch the floor with the beaters.

Many of the patients are not able to follow a steady beat, and some can't concentrate.

It is difficult for most of the patients to clap their hands. Many have fixed hand positions . . . such as cramped fingers, or a hand that is slightly closed all the time.

By doing isolated movements, the patient is made aware of the different parts of his body . . .

First he touches . . .

Then he moves . . . head . . . shoulders . .

Often when the patient attempts to lift a shoulder, he lifts the elbows, or the hand, or the entire body.

He moves his hands . . . feet . . . legs.

It is important to do stretches. They increase the possibilities of coordination . . . They increase the range of movement . . . And they help the patients open out.

The stretches often start with a basic rocking action.

To restore the balance between the two most extreme positions . . . the closed-in and the opened-out . . . the class is given several variations of these two positions.

It is important that a closed-in person should experience an open and extended position . . . and that an opened-out person should eventually become aware of a closed-in position.

During the class, the patients are periodically encouraged to inspect . . . to look . . . to accept.

It is necessary, and incidentally very enjoyable, for the patient to reexperience some of the movements of childhood . . . such as gallops, jumps, hops, turns and skips.

These patients are usually afraid to express themselves freely. Perhaps they may have suffered for having expressed themselves *too freely*. Instead of asking them to show anger, affection, or any other emotional expressions, they are given the movements or forms that are universally known and used for these expressions, such as . . . throwing, kicking, stamping in anger, or caressing with affection. It seems that fulfilling the *movement* tends to reawaken the corresponding emotion and feeling.

Scarves and other props are used to help the patients vary the quality of movement.

The texture and color of the scarves seem to be of great importance.

The class is encouraged and inspired by the teacher.

They are also encouraged to do individual improvisation. They enjoy doing this, but it often takes a certain amount of individual encouragement to get them started.

A most significant objective is to develop the patient's awareness of others, and to help him accept others.

Because movement is not a lasting statement and since it is not recorded, it relieves the patient of the responsibilities that are sometimes involved in other forms of expression.

Whether we are teaching children or adults, we call upon the basic movement forms of life. We call upon the basic emotional feelings of life. We call upon the rhythms of life. We use these movements, emotions and rhythms in making a social contact, in facilitating the free expression of emotion, in creating self-awareness and a clear personal identity. We use them to help develop what is already there, and we use them to guide the patients into a framework of control and balance and true freedom of expression.

INDEX